MINISTRY 3.0

How Today's Church Leaders Are Using Coaching to Transform Ministry

Compiled by J. Val Hastings, MCC

Cathedral Rose Books, the Christian Imprint of
Love Your Life Publishing
St. Peters, Mo 63376
636-922-2634

ISBN: 978-1-934509-54-8
Library of Congress Control Number: 2012943851
Printed in the United States of America and Great Britian
First Printing 2012

Cover design: www.Cyanotype.ca
Editing by Linda Dessau and Gwen Hoffnagle

DEDICATION

This book is dedicated to Jesus, the Master Coach.

2 Timothy 1:6 & 7

Therefore I remind you to stir up the gift that is within you . . . for God has not given us a spirit of fear, but of power and of love and of a sound mind.

ACKNOWLEDGEMENTS

Each contributing author has someone who first introduced us to coaching and encouraged us to go further with it. Thank you for getting us started on our own coaching journeys. You coached, trained and mentored us so that we could each write our contributions to this book. We appreciate your influence on us.

A special thank you to the authors who contributed chapters to this book; the depth and breadth of your chapters is tremendous. Thank you for your invaluable offerings to this book. Thank you to (in alphabetical order):

- Teresa Angle-Young
- Dave Biser
- Nancy M. Stefano
- Don Eisenhauer
- Ed George
- Michael Godfrey
- Ed Hale
- David P. Hyatt
- Kay L. Kotan
- Jim Latimer
- Larry Ousley
- Claire Pedrick
- Sue Politte
- Jim Robey
- C. Darrell Roland
- Patricia Suggs
- Jennifer Williams

To my online business manager and virtual assistant, Laura Pumo, and her team at Office DEVA, thank you for pulling this all together for me. Your assistance was invaluable.

To our editor, Linda Dessau, working with you was one of the best decisions I ever made with my business. Thank you for bringing our ideas to light and helping us clarify and polish our messages.

To our project manager and publisher, Lynne Klippel, thank you for your practical help in turning this into an actual book. Your help made this feel effortless and enjoyable.

To all of the pastors, ministry staff, and church leaders that we, as contributing authors, have coached and trained, this book is filled with what you have taught us. Others will benefit from your experiences and wisdom.

Table of Contents

Introduction
by J. Val Hastings

Before You Read This Book

"If the 1950s ever return, the church is well-equipped and ready." In recent years I've heard several pastors and ministry leaders make this statement. It's usually followed by laughter among the pastors in the room, including me! We all get it. The models of ministry that many are using are outdated and ineffective in today's world. In fact, several of the models are so antiquated that it is truly laughable.

This book is for after the laughter. It's an anthology for those who are ready to consider new ways of being in ministry – ways that are actually effective. It is written expressly for those willing to embrace new models of ministry.

I was recently challenged by a ministry leader about this whole idea of the need for a new model and way of being in ministry. He really took offense at what he called "business language" – terms such as *outcome*, *results*, and effectiveness. Here's what he wrote, "Success in ministry is defined by obedience, not by results." With my coach hat on I followed up with, "How's that going for you?" I was saddened, but not surprised, when he wrote back that his church would probably be closing later this year.

Please understand that I agree that ministry is about obedience and commitment, but to the core components of Christianity, not to a model or framework. The Tarrant Baptist Association in Ft. Worth, Texas was an early adopter of a coaching approach to ministry. Years ago I asked them why that was, and I will never forget what they told me: "We decided a long time ago that we would do whatever it takes to be faithful to the Great Commission, even if that meant completely changing the way we do ministry."

Strap yourself in. This will be new material for most of you. This book is filled with much more than information about coaching. These chapters will "prime the pump" as you prayerfully consider shifting out of a 1950's model of ministry and into something entirely new, exciting *and* effective.

Some of you probably think coaching is just a fad. Yet today coaching has worked its way into the mainstream of some of today's biggest and most influential corporations at every professional level and every area of expertise, not to mention health and other intimate personal issues. Whatever skill, mindset, or goal you're aiming for, there's a coach for that. This is no fad.

Coaching is what you didn't get in seminary. But it's what you wanted.

Why this anthology was created

Throughout my years of providing coaching and coach training to pastors, ministry staff, and church leaders, a recurring response has surfaced: "Hey, this is great stuff, how do I use it?" This book comes in response to that common curiosity amongst many in ministry. Just how are people using these coaching techniques in real life ministry settings?

This resource was designed to give you solid examples of coaching in ministry, and we even provide you the contact information of the contributing authors so that you can reach them directly and learn even more.

I believe this is one of those books that pastors and ministry leaders will want to keep close by and refer to regularly. We've already decided that this book will be required reading for our coach training students at Coaching4Clergy.

The other rationale for creating this book was to highlight the people who are doing this well. It is such a privilege for me to introduce these contributing coaches and to applaud their work in a very public way. In the tradition of Benjamin Zander, they all get an "A."

I know each contributing coach in this book, and I've seen them all in action. Over the past several months it has been my privilege to review their individual chapter contributions multiple times, and I have gleaned much from what they offer. I'm confident that you will learn much from reading their contributions, and even more when you follow up with those you are drawn to.

What I hope you will get from this book

Whether you are ordained or not, I am hoping that by reading this book you will be inspired, moved to action and empowered to make changes; that you will pull out ideas, learn new concepts and be able to apply them in your own familiar context.

At its core, coaching is about empowering others. What if empowering and equipping people became the norm in your faith community? Consider the impact that your faith community could have locally and globally. And so ultimately, I hope reading this book leads to your Next Great Awakening of that reality.

The power of stories

This is not a skill-building book, this is a different approach – an approach straight from the Bible. The Bible is full of stories. Pastors tell stories from the pulpit all the time. This book contains real stories from the trenches; this is not theory. And you'll not only see the successes, you'll hear about challenges where the rubber hit the road, and how these extraordinary coaches found their way through them.

With 6 out of 10 churches doomed to close in the next 10 years, this book is a ray of hope for what can be.

What is Ministry 3.0?

You may be wondering about the title, "Ministry 3.0." The concept follows what we see in the computer world, every time Microsoft or some other company releases a new version of their software. With this update, you're not just getting a few simple tweaks and some bug fixes; this is a whole new package to install. In terms of ministry, we are at one of those places where *the platelets are really shifting.* It's not about doing what we've been doing better, it's about a whole new approach – a coaching approach – through which we're really empowering all people.

Ministry 1.0 was when Jesus was alive, and during the formation of the early church. Ministry 2.0 began when Augustine in Rome made Christianity the religion of the people, and then continued with Martin Luther and the Protestant Reformation. Which bring us to the 1950s.

In many ways, Ministry 3.0 is a re-emergence of Ministry 1.0 – an empowering of all of God's people. Reggie McNeal refers to this as the New Reformation, which is about freeing God's people from the institution called "the church" (Reggie McNeal, *The Present Future*, page 43).

Why Does Ministry Need to be Transformed?

Churches are closing, membership is shrinking, and pastors feel alone and unsupported. One online article from August 2010 by Eugene Cho even called it "death by ministry" – a striking account of the emotional and mental stressors of ministry today.

And what's more, congregants aren't having their needs met. "They are not leaving [the church] because they have lost faith. They are leaving the church to preserve their faith." (Reggie McNeal, *The Present Future*, page 4.)

What Is Coaching?

Let me explain that if coaching is completely new to you, this book will not teach you how to be a coach. It will not even teach you, in so many words, what coaching is. What this book will do is inspire you with the miracles that coaching can invite. And when that happens, I suggest your next step be to visit http://coaching4clergy.com/find-a-coach/find-a-coach/ to book a complimentary session and experience coaching for yourself.

You can also refer to our other coaching books (http://coaching4clergy.com/products/coaching-books/) and training programs (http://coaching4clergy.com/coaching-programs/) for more possibilities.

Who is Coaching4Clergy? Who is J. Val Hastings?

Coaching4Clergy provides coach training programs for pastors, church leaders, and ministry staff. When I first experienced coaching for myself, I remember thinking, "What if I adopted a coaching approach to ministry?

What if the larger church adopted a coaching approach to ministry?" In that moment a vision began to emerge – a global vision of every pastor, ministry staff, and church leader a coach.

That's the vision of Coaching4Clergy. Those eight simple words: Every pastor, ministry staff, and church leader a coach.

Those eight simple words have the ability to radically transform the local church and its leaders. It's the next great awakening in Christianity. It's Ministry 3.0.

I'm one of those crazy individuals who believe that we can change the world, and my contribution is to make certain that everyone in ministry has coaching skills in their toolkit.

Aside from being founder and president of Coaching4Clergy, I am the author of The Next Great Awakening: How to Empower God's People with a Coach Approach to Ministry, and the e-book The E3-Church: Empowered, Effective and Entrepreneurial Leadership That Will Keep Your Church Alive. I hold the designation of master certified coach through the International Coach Federation, the highest coaching designation.

Who You Will Meet in This Book

Our authors are pastors and ministry leaders, coaches and trainers, former pastors and former executives. They come from a diverse cross-section of small towns and big cities, the one common thread being that they have all found a way to effectively apply a coaching approach to ministry.

I intentionally invited this eclectic group of contributors to be part of this book to demonstrate that you do not need to be ordained to transform your church, nor do you need to have a church or association of a certain size. I want to empower each of you reading this book to create your own success stories.

The Themes

Ministry 3.0 is divided into four themes. You are welcome to read the entire book from start to finish, or to dive into the section that first grabs your interest. Some of the stories overlap more than one theme, so please be sure to read them all eventually.

As your own experience, skill set, and ministry settings evolve, certain stories will become more relevant to you. Please keep this book handy – if you're facing a challenge using coaching in ministry, it's likely that one of our authors has addressed it.

Section One: Practical Help for Pastors – These stories describe how coaching can assist pastors with their day-to-day duties in different aspects of ministry.

Section Two: Leadership and Team Development – These stories highlight coaching as a leadership tool and demonstrate how coaching can smooth out group dynamics and capitalize on the strengths of a group.

Section Three: Major Change and Transition, Multi-Sites, and New Church Sites – These stories explore change, growth, and segmentation, and how coaching can ease the way into these unknown territories.

Section Four: Creating a Larger Coaching Culture – Coaching cannot exist in a vacuum, and so these stories explain how to weave coaching into the core activities, mindsets, and interactions in a ministry setting.

The Time is Here

Your work in ministry compels you to serve God's people. In Ministry 3.0, you'll witness an expanded vision of how you can transform that work to have a greater impact on the people you serve and a greater level of satisfaction for you personally.

God's richest blessings to you as you read this book and apply its powerful message.

J. Val Hastings,
September, 2012

Proverbs 20:5

The purposes of a person's heart are deep waters, but a man of understanding draws them out.

SECTION ONE:

Practical Help for Pastors

During the twenty-plus years that I pastored local churches, I was always looking for resources and practical help for the day-to-day pastoral work that I did. No sooner had I preached a sermon, when it seemed like it was already time to preach the next sermon. Determined not to deliver a "Saturday night special," I was most grateful for sermon suggestions. It was the same with weekly Bible studies and special seasons of the year. On top of that, there were always the growing pastoral care needs and requests for help.

This section contains examples of practical pastoral help covering a wide range of areas from preaching and teaching to pastoral care and special seasons. There is even a chapter to help you improve your focus and effectiveness.

One of the tenets of coaching is that the coachee does the work. As you read through these chapters, consider letting go of the need as ministry leader to do all the work or be the expert. Instead, experience the freedom and joy that come from drawing out and empowering others. Yes, as ministry leaders we have a role and responsibility; and so do others.

Fishing for a Different Fish: Using Scripture in Coaching

By *Jim Robey*

"What does this remind you of from the Bible?" That powerful question asked by my coach had a major impact on me. Suddenly I was connecting my coachable moment with a personal favorite Bible story. While exploring my story and that Bible story, I uncovered a spiritual connection that supported me in taking an important action in my life. And I discovered a new metaphor for my work as a coach.

My metaphor? Fishing for a different "fish."

I was gripped by the story of Jesus's call to Peter and Andrew found in Matthew 4:18-20. Jesus invited them to leave their fishing nets behind and follow him, and they would "fish" for men and women. They would leave the security of the known for the unknown. In 2004, because of my connection to this story, I determined that my call is to follow Jesus; not as a pastor, but as a coach to other pastors.

For thirty-five years I had been a pastor of local churches. Just like Peter and Andrew, I was invited leave my nets (the local church ministry) to follow Jesus and fish for people (coach pastors and church leaders). This was, using a phrase from Mother Teresa, a "call within a call." I did not have a clear vision of what this would be, and there were very few models available at that time. What I knew deep within my soul was that this was what I was to do now. My then sixteen-year-old daughter expressed it this way: "You are leaving a perfectly good job with a perfectly good salary for a position that does not exist and no money." This fishing metaphor took on even more meaning as I moved to the Alabama Gulf Coast to live.

Coaches often work with metaphors. Metaphors are like mirrors, reflecting our inner images of self, life, and others. They may be drawn from poems, literature, music, TV, or movies. The Bible's stories, images, and passages are also sources for metaphors. The coachee – the person being coached – is invited to find what is valuable and meaningful for him or her. A Biblical metaphor might provide that deep connection. By connecting the coachee with the scripture, the coach can allow the "aha!" to occur. This is the place in the coaching process where the Holy Spirit may be most at work. Here the coachee is able to deepen the learning and move forward in taking the action she or he is choosing.

Using scripture in coaching is about exploring the story, image, or passage together with the coachee. A co-active approach allows room for the Holy Spirit to be active. As the coach, it's not about my telling or directing; it's about the coachee and me considering and reflecting together on the chosen metaphor. Although I might have an intuition about what may be useful, I am often surprised by what story, image, or passage the person chooses. What makes it so meaningful for the coachee is that it is his or her choice. Sometimes the person feels stumped and asks for my help. Then I may offer a passage or image that comes to my mind. However, if my suggestion doesn't work for the person, I let it go. I hold my suggestions lightly, as one might a feather. It is not what speaks to me as coach, but what speaks to the coachee that is important.

During my years of coaching, I have crafted a basic question that invites my coachees to explore their situation using a Biblical story, image, or passage. There is power in the moment as they become conscious of the similarity between their situation and the Biblical metaphor. I might ask:

- "So, what Biblical stories come to mind that could be helpful/ similar/useful?"
- "So, what story from the scriptures speaks to you?
- "What image from the Bible comes to your mind?
- "If you were to choose a verse of scripture to aid you in this moment, what would it be?

Here are three things to remember when using metaphor from scripture:

1. **<u>Invite</u>** the coachee to share the connection he or she is experiencing. After all, it's all about the coachee, not about you as the coach.

Ways to do this include brainstorming together, asking about a favorite passage, or musing, "I wonder what Jesus might say if he were here?" The coach can also inquire about recent devotional readings, journal writings, and worship experiences to allow a connection to the Bible. Pay attention to what question brings a "wow" response.

2. **Explore** the passage and what it might reveal about a particular situation in the coachee's life. Explore the revelation by talking through multiple thoughts and possibilities. Look at it from at least three different perspectives. What lesson can be taken away from the discussion and applied to the person's life now? Next, remember to ask the AWE question: And what else? This allows even more insight and connection by catching any final insights that might be lurking.

3. **Apply a reminder**. The learning for the coachee can be enhanced by her or his choosing something tangible to aid in remembering this connection. It might be a symbol, song, picture, smell, movement, or item. What gives this real power for the coachee is that it is clearly spoken and chosen by him or her. I often ask, "What will help you remember this scriptural metaphor?" Here are some real-life examples:

   - Abi chose a "competency coin" to remind her that God had already created her to be competent for her work of ministry.

   - Dale chose a passage from Philippians 4:13 (NKJV) – "I can do all things through Christ who strengthens me" – as he dealt with a challenging situation in his congregation.

   - A favorite picture of Jesus carrying a sheep aided Dolores to remember and claim her beloved-ness as a child of God.

   - Keith added the song *On Eagles' Wings* to his daily devotions as a way to reconnect to God's providential care for him and his family in a time of uncertainty.

   - John, a businessman, placed a Bible on his desk as a reminder that all of his life was God's, and that his desire was to serve God through his work.

- The gesture of cupped hands (as to receive a gift) was what Alan chose as he experienced a great abundance of successes in his life.

- Mary wore her favorite cross, which had a new specific meaning for her, while making the decision about moving to another congregation.

Coaches can also use scripture in group coaching with ministry leaders and church staff teams. Again, asking powerful questions allows coachees to connect their current realities to their spiritual resources. I like to ask:

- What Biblical story is important for us to remember in this moment?
- If we could only keep one passage of scripture to guide us in this situation, which one would we select?
- Using the scriptures of this liturgical season, what theme is emerging for our ministry?
- What from the Book of _____ applies to our church now?
- How does this apply to you personally as part of this ministry team?

For me, the use of scripture in coaching can be a powerful place of learning and action. The use of scripture as metaphor encourages a spiritual connection to develop, and a coachee may be shaped, formed, and transformed by the scripture. Through this process an individual's faith may be enhanced and deepened. As a coach I am unattached to the story or metaphor, allowing it to be a place of fulfillment for the coachee. This is where Jesus's words in John 10:10 bring special meaning to me as he says, "I came so that they could have life – indeed, so that they could live life to the fullest." (CEV) This is so true for me and my ministry of coaching. I have discovered that in my call to follow Jesus and coach others, I experience living life to the fullest.

What three lessons are you taking away from this chapter? Write them down here.

1.

2.

3.

And finally, what story from scripture are *you* living now?

~~~~~~~~~~~~~~~~~~~~~~~~~

Dr. Jim Robey, a United Methodist minister and professional certified coach, is the global coaching initiative coordinator for **Coaching4Clergy**. He was the first UMC clergyperson to be officially endorsed for Ministry of Life Coaching. Jim is a renowned speaker, pastor, seminar leader, teacher, and coach, with a profound commitment to helping others grow in their ministry and connection to God.

He earned his Doctor of Ministry degree from Emory University in Atlanta, Georgia, and is a graduate of the Co-Active Leadership Program of the Coaches Training Institute in California. Jim coaches ministers, laypersons, and church leaders from many different denominations who are motivated to grow in life and ministry. An avid global traveler who once worked with Mother Teresa in Calcutta, Jim brings a passion for equipping new leaders for the world-wide church. Jim and his wife, Betty, live in Gulf Shores, Alabama, near the Gulf of Mexico. They are blessed with two daughters, one son-in-law, two grandchildren, and two dogs.

jim.robey@coaching4clergy.com
~~~~~~~~~~~~~~~~~~~~~~~~~

Navigating the Path: Coaching Relationships

By *C. Darrell Roland*

John and Julianne

In late June, 2010, John and Julianne hit a wall in their marriage. While it was not a bad marriage, they just felt stuck and desired more in their relationship. They had been to counselors, but continued to struggle in moving forward. Julianne remembered reading an article in a local magazine about marriage written by a relationship coach. They contacted the magazine and asked them to review their back issues to find the coach's contact information. After making an initial call, they had their first session.

Their coaches were Charles and Sandy. Charles was the author of the article and Sandy was his wife. Charles and Sandy began the session by sharing the differences between coaching and counseling, and how the coaching process would flow. John and Julianne learned that coaching would create an environment in which they could build their own pathway to the marriage they desired. They left the session refreshed and eager to move forward. Over the next few sessions, they built a plan to help them move their marriage from good to great. Their newfound invigoration reignited their passions and dreams. They felt empowered to draw their own blueprint of marriage. Over the next several months, John and Julianne moved their marriage to a better place than it had ever been.

Daniel

It was 6:30 a.m. on a cold Tuesday morning in October when Aaron walked into the kitchen to get his morning coffee and begin his quiet time. Passing by the front window, he noticed a white car parked on the street. With a closer look, he saw his son Daniel sitting in the driver's seat. Daniel normally left for work at 5:00 a.m. What was he doing sitting in his car, staring at nothing? He walked outside and approached the car. Daniel rolled down the window and said, "Dad, I just got let go from my job." Daniel's company laid off fifteen managers. He'd only been promoted to manager a few months prior to the layoffs. "Dad," he continued, "I'm trying to get my life on track with God and now this happens."

Daniel was twenty-eight and had recently experienced a difficult divorce from a verbally and emotionally abusive wife. Because of this, he was living with his parents until he could get re-established. He was already feeling as if he had failed as a husband, father, and man, and now he felt that he'd failed in his career. This was a major blow, and he really had no idea where to go from there.

After several days of emotional release and a couple weeks of calming, Daniel approached Aaron, who was a coach, and asked if he would help him. Aaron and Daniel began a journey of coaching within the context of their relationship. They spent hours simply discussing what was in Daniel's heart that aligned with his gifts. These coaching conversations allowed Daniel to dream again. Daniel built a plan from his ideas and desires that led him to articulate his ideal work setting in which he would be able to say, "Today I am getting paid to play all day." He has found this place and is thriving instead of striving.

Coaching Approach in Relationships

Relationships can be challenging to navigate, sometimes leaving us feeling lost and confused. Coaching skills can provide a roadmap that helps us avoid going down the wrong path. The stories above are examples of how coaching can enrich relationships and lives.

The following are the skills and characteristics that I include when I'm training others to be relationship coaches. Some will seem obvious, and others may just lead to some "aha!" moments. All of them are essential for successful coaching.

Create an environment of trust

- Model it rather than expect it
- Be safe, supportive, and approachable at all times

Be open and transparent

- Be authentic and share personal examples at strategic times
- Be open to self-awareness by having your own coach

Be present

- Listen at all levels: eyes, tones, and what's not said
- Ensure clarity by reframing and restating

Cultivate intimacy

- Discuss various types of intimacy
- Have fun together and laugh together

Help everyone become better

- Encourage, edify, and identify the fuel for maintaining the momentum
- Dream courageously, and expect great things

Marriage Coaching

The marriage relationship comes with a few distinct nuances that require some additional techniques. Here are some key areas to really focus on when coaching couples:

Create the trust environment by clearly stating confidentiality and living by it. You will also need to subtly establish your credibility, without focusing on you. Married couples appreciate knowing that their coaches also understand the dynamics of marriage. Also, it is essential to keep the environment free from all judgment, facilitating trust and evoking openness on the part of the couple.

Identify the integrity of the relationship by reviewing the relational architecture that built the current state of their marriage. This will help them identify who they are and where they've been. Take a short amount of time to discuss the current habits and hang-ups of their relationship, but you don't want to spend much time here; it is only to help create awareness of who and where they are now.

Look at their present path's end point by using powerful questions that create new awareness around the outcome of taking no action. This will lay the platform for you to share the positive benefits and value of marriage coaching.

Identify their desired outcome, which will allow you to define the coaching relationship and the coaching agreement. This will help them understand the coaching process and that the ownership of the outcome is truly theirs.

Help them paint their path by encouraging them to visualize their desired outcome. Push them to paint their most magnificent picture of their desired marriage. Then ask them to come up with a visual symbol to keep them focused on that picture. Now is the time to incorporate new practices and actions to take them to a new place, and identify how they will get there.

Follow up and follow through by helping them create checkpoints and accountability. During this process, be sure to celebrate with them. They need to feel the wins to maintain the momentum. After arriving at their new exciting place, encourage them to share their newfound marriage fulfillment with others. This will tap in to the power of the testimony and plant positive seeds in others, resulting in expediential fruit for all.

Additional Relationship Coaching Tips:

- Don't try to do more than coaching. Refer out as necessary.
- Keep it about the coachee's forward movement.
- Always believe in the best *in* your coachees and *about* your coachees.
- Never judge, criticize, or condemn at any time.
- Be sincerely interested in your coachee and your coachee's welfare.

- Be honest, respectful, and constructive.
- Keep proper personal boundaries in place.
- Always come prepared and be present for your coachee.
- Model the relational practices you speak about.
- Be professional in all aspects of the coaching relationship.
- Define your availability and always be approachable.
- Follow through with your role and follow up on your coachee's responsibilities.
- Acknowledge positive progress and celebrate successes with your coachee.
- Be thankful for and appreciative of each coachee as a person.
- Never use your coaching skills to manipulate.
- Don't coach toward the end you see, only toward your coachee's desired end.
- Stick to scheduled time slots and length of sessions.
- Regularly calibrate your progress as a coach and your coachee's progress.
- Want more for your coachees than they want for themselves.
- Listen to what is not said as much what is said.
- Tell stories and use metaphors to paint pictures.
- Don't let your coachees settle. Push them to become who they desire to be.
- Learn each coachee's communication style to ensure you are speaking his or her language.
- Find the connection point that will bridge the coachee to you as the coach.
- Always point coachees forward, not backward.
- Listen to that still, small voice.
- Reassure your coachees that you are there and God is there for them.
- Pray for your coachees on a regular basis, including before and after each session.
- Always give God the glory for what He does in your coachees' lives.

~~~~~~~~~~~~~~~~~~~~~~~~~~~~
~~~~~~~~~~~~~~~~~~~~~~~~~~~~

C. Darrell Roland, PCC, CCA, spent twenty years in industrial and corporate environments prior to moving into ministry, where he has served the past eleven years as an executive pastor for a growing multi-site church. He became a certified church administrator through the National Association of Church Business Administration (NACBA) and Candler Theological Institute. He completed his coaching studies with Coach U and Coaching4Clergy, and he is accredited as a professional certified coach with the International Coach Federation. He serves as faculty at Coaching4Clergy, where he is a trainer, class facilitator, coach, and mentor coach to pastors and ministry leaders.

Darrell is co-founder of Red Pin Ministries where he and his team serve churches in a variety of areas including accounting services, consulting, strategy, vision, and organizational structure.

darrell.roland@Coaching4Clergy.com

Stressless Preaching: How Coaching Helps Pastors to Preach with Power

By Teresa Angle-Young

Mark sat before me, anxiously folding, unfolding, and then refolding a piece of paper as he spoke. "I just don't have anything new to say about this text. I've preached this scripture at least ten times in my career. There is nothing new under the sun." I could feel his anxiety and frustration; could see the tension on his face, in his body, and in the sound of his voice. "I'm just worn out. I'm not a creative guy. I'm a workhorse, and I love my people, but I am simply out of ideas."

"Tell me how you prepare for a sermon," I began. Mark sighed deeply and then said, "Well, on Monday morning I come into my office here at the church and read over the text." He paused. "Then I start reading some of my commentaries about the passage." He shifted uncomfortably in his seat. "Then I just start praying." He looked at me and laughed nervously. "That goes on most of the week, in between appointments, meetings, and the usual crises, until about Friday, which is supposed to be my 'day off.' At that point I either start to panic, or just find a sermon online that I can pretty much copy. Or sometimes I just go in on Sunday morning with some sort of rough outline or idea, and hope that the Holy Spirit will fill in the blanks!"

I looked at Mark for a moment. "And what usually happens?" I asked. Mark chuckled wryly. "That depends. Sometimes I luck out. Other times I feel as if I'm either just rambling, or spouting the same old platitudes that have stopped meaning anything, and it sort of falls flat." "How does that feel?" I asked. "Most of the time I walk out of church on Sunday feeling a little disappointed in myself, wondering if God spoke to anyone through me that day," he said sadly.

We sat for a moment, and then I asked, "Mark, how would you *like* to feel on Sunday after church?" Mark stared down at the myriad of paperwork on his desk, at the pile of unopened mail, the stack of pink slips with calls to be returned, and the large worn leather Bible, and he sighed deeply. "I would like to feel as if the words of my mouth and the meditations of my heart had helped someone know Christ." I smiled.

~~~~~~~~~~~~~~~~~~~~~~~~~

A seminary student stumbled into my office with a book bag, computer case, purse, and a couple of preaching books, plopped down in a chair, then announced that in preparing to preach for the first time, she was as "lost as Henny Penny!" In reviewing her exegetical work, I could see evidence of excellent preparation. In reviewing her homiletical work, I could see evidence of about twenty-seven sermon ideas. So what was the problem? She only needed to write one sermon, and she only had ten minutes to preach it!

"I just don't know where to start!" she gushed. "I have a million ideas but I can't seem to focus on one. How do I start to narrow this down, and how do I know what anyone wants to hear anyway?"

One of these preachers had lots of experience and no creative ideas. The other one had no experience and no focus. Both preachers were feeling frustrated. Neither seemed in touch with either the needs or desires of their mission field, and neither seemed to know how to truly, deeply, genuinely connect with the richness of the text in a profoundly personal way.

For preachers who follow the Revised Common Lectionary, the choice of sermon text is narrow. For preachers who develop their own sermon series or choose their own text, it is easy to pick familiar passages or find online resources for sermon outlines. Unfortunately, often the preacher either develops a too-narrow canon of favorite scriptures, or discovers that the
~~~~~~~~~~~~~~~~~~~~~~~~~

canned online resources do not resonate with either their personal style or the real spiritual needs of their congregations.

For the preacher who is new to the pulpit, preaching can be an intimidating and sometimes overwhelming experience. For the seasoned preacher, preaching can become unimaginative and routine. Some preachers *write* great sermons but have a delivery that is as dry as unbuttered toast. Others are engaging and eloquent, but offer little substance in the sermon. For every pastor, finding ways to preach the Word in fresh, authentic ways is a challenge.

Great preaching is transformative for the listener and a benchmark of vital congregations. The good news is that every preacher, regardless of experience, education, age, or other circumstances, can be coached to place greater comfort and effectiveness in their preaching.

Here are some key issues to address during these coaching sessions:

How do you typically prepare your sermon?

Coachable insights:

- Is the preacher overwhelmed with other responsibilities? If so, how can the preacher delegate, then disengage with those responsibilities?
- Is the preacher allowing time and space to hear God's Word? Are there health or wellness issues present? Personal issues? Church conflicts?
- Has the preacher internalized the text in order for relevant illustrations to become apparent? In other words, is the preacher reading the text, praying the text, breathing the text, and living the text? What practices might enrich the preacher's reading of the text?

How do you feel about this text? What are the key words or phrases that jump out when you read it?

Coachable insights:

- Is the text more than just sermon fodder?

- What is the preacher's view of scripture?
- Is the preacher struggling with his or her own faith?
- How does the preacher see the text alive in the world?
- How has the preacher experienced this text in everyday life?

What are the concerns of your community, and of your congregation?

Coachable insights:

- Is the preacher in touch with the congregation?
- Does the preacher know the mission field?
- Is there hurt, anger, resentment, or other negative emotions that stand between the preacher and the congregation?

In the coaching setting, issues often arise that seem peripheral to the preaching experience, but careful listening and clarification may reveal limiting beliefs, fears, and insecurities. The coach can then brainstorm with and support the preacher in finding and developing new practices – approaches to preaching that will allow God to use the text to speak to the preacher in fresh ways and with clarity and focus for the needs of the congregation. In this way, the overall spiritual health of the preacher is honored and affirmed, as the preacher is able to rest in the scripture and find deep personal meaning in the text. Preaching is also enriched as he or she finds new ways to connect the Word to the life experiences of the congregation.

Through coaching, the text often *comes alive* for the preacher in ways that make for relevant, engaging, and powerful preaching experiences. Coaching the preacher involves deep listening as the coach assesses the emotional barometer of the preacher and encourages the preacher to clarify and brainstorm ideas for the sermon. The discovery process may also reveal that the preacher needs and wants to create space in their busy schedule for reading, reflection, and personal spiritual development, all of which benefit sermon preparation and delivery.

The following tips may help your coachees to experience stressless preaching.

How to Preach with Power

Make time and space for relaxed and deep engagement with the text. Schedule this on your calendar just as you would any other important event each week.

Listen deeply to your congregation, and then allow the text to speak to you in relevant ways. What is God saying through the text to your people this week?

Pay attention to your own spiritual and emotional health. Are you resting into the text? Are you rested enough to give energy to your exegesis? Are you a living embodiment of the sermon? *How is your soul?*

How can you improve the delivery of your sermon? Can your congregation hear you, see you, and understand you clearly? Are you relaxed and confident? Are you fully present in the moment of worship? Does your sermon have good news for you?

Powerful preaching facilitates an encounter with Christ, and is one of the primary ways that our congregations connect with God. Powerful preaching answers the "So what?" question of the scripture for the congregation. And powerful preaching is a mark of a healthy congregation and a healthy preacher. Through coaching, every preacher can become one who speaks with power, authority, compassion, and love.

~~~~~~~~~~~~~~~~~~~~~~~~~~~

The Reverend **Teresa Angle-Young** is a United Methodist pastor and church planter in Atlanta, Georgia. She holds a B.A. in English from the University of Tennessee, a M. Div. from Emory University, and is finishing a D. Min. in preaching at Aquinas Institute of Theology. Her dissertation is on preaching to postmoderns. Teresa coaches and consults with church planters, preachers, and speakers. You can find resources and learn more at www.stresslesspreaching.com.
~~~~~~~~~~~~~~~~~~~~~~~~~~~

Letting Go and Taking Up: Lenten Spiritual Coaching

by *Nancy DeStefano*

It was in the fourth week of coaching that Anna realized the job she was about to start was not going to be one that would be healthy for her. Like the job before it and the one before that, she was setting herself up to be disappointed again as she struggled to be someone she was not and to do tasks that did not fit her being. By the sixth coaching call, Anna had decided to refuse the job, continue her leave of absence, and seek a new direction in her life. By week eight, as our Lenten spiritual coaching came to a close, Anna was searching out schools that would help her prepare for a career in a new field – one that would touch her heart and give her the opportunity to be engaged in work that was meaningful to her and in keeping with who she was and who God was calling her to be.

When I began planning for the Lenten Spiritual Journey coaching program, I didn't know what to expect. I hoped that it would touch people's lives with God's love and they would find a new and deeper relationship with Christ. I hoped that the Lenten season would infuse the coaching with the idea of letting go – giving up whatever needs to be given up and taking up whatever needs to be taken up – in order to be fully alive. I knew that each person's Lenten journey would be unique to them. No prescription was planned. The coaching experience was to be unique to each coachee – as unique as the coachee himself or herself.

For that reason the calls were very fluid in design. Each call began with a time of quieting and centering, deeply breathing in the love of God while letting go of the cares and anxieties that might be weighing us down and keeping us from hearing the still, small voice of God. Each call ended with a prayer and a scripture reading – sometimes chosen by the coach, sometimes by the coachee – to assist the coachee in their prayer time during the upcoming week.

In between, each call took on the unique character of each caller. Each coachee wanted to grow closer to God; some wanted to discern God's call on their lives, some wanted to live more fully as the people they were created to be, some wanted to delve into their relationships with their family, friends, or vocation, and others were looking to deepen their prayer life or try out new spiritual disciplines that they hoped would help center them more fully in God's presence.

Anna was experiencing the anxiety and discomfort of trying to be someone she was not. She felt that she should be looking forward to her new position. She thought that her anxiety was due only to the unknowns that come with any new job experience. I asked about what she hoped for in this new job, what she imagined it would be like, and what the stumbling blocks to success were for her. As we delved more deeply into her situation, Anna began to feel more and more that this was not simply anxiety about something new, but about a wrong fit between who she was and what the job would ask of her. She began to recognize that this job was filled with all the problems and concerns that she had left behind in her last position, and that if she took it she would simply be repeating old patterns and be just as unhappy as she had been before. A *strengths inventory* helped her to pinpoint her gifts and discern what qualities God had graced her with that she might make use of in seeking new directions for her ministry.

Linda came to the Lenten Spiritual Journey coaching program seeking a more positive relationship with her children. She felt that her work was taking her away from the time she should be giving to them, and she wanted to reassess her commitments and her lifestyle. There was a gap between what she was doing and what she wanted to be doing. This gap extended to her relationship with God and her relationship with her family. Through coaching we were able to map out her options and work through time management issues that would give her time for her work – which was important to her, time for her family life – which gave her great joy, and time for God – which grounded and centered her for all the other aspects of her life.

Colin was deeply involved in his church and in social justice movements that were important to him. He had an important position in his denomination as a layperson. He was seeking to become more deeply centered in God's Word and in God's call on his life. As part of our coaching, we read a book about the spiritual journey that took us through Christ's journey to Jerusalem and the cross. At times Colin felt that he was beyond the content of the book. Through questioning, he discovered that he was putting up a block because of his dislike for being out of control. He was not allowing God to be in control of his life, and he was not giving himself as totally to his faith as he thought he was. Through this insight, we walked together through the book, and he found himself more able to trust in God's grace and strength and to rely less on trying to control everything and everyone in his life.

Matt wanted to try out different forms of spiritual practices and prayer. After asking questions about what he was seeking, what had worked for him in the past, and what obstacles he thought might lie ahead, we experimented with several different spiritual practices and disciplines. We worked on *lectio divina*, meditation, and centering prayer. We used the Daily Office and other forms of daily prayer. We also worked through fasting and what that could mean in our spiritual growth. Matt found Lenten disciplines that he said he would incorporate into that season from then on, and he found new prayer forms for all year long.

For Jennifer, life was moving along pretty well, but it seemed like something was missing. When I asked where she experienced the gap between what she believed God wanted for her life and where she was in the present, she found it nearly impossible to say. We worked through the Wheel of Life exercise that assesses how well each aspect of one's life is going. Through that exercise, Jennifer realized that there were several parts of her life in which there was a gap between where she wanted to be and where she currently was. Through more questioning, Jennifer discovered ways to find more peace and consolation in areas of her life that had previously felt out of whack.

The Lenten Spiritual Journey coaching program was comprised of eight weeks of coaching – one hour per week – for a set fee. The eight weeks began the week of Ash Wednesday and continued through the week after Easter. The experience invited participants on a pilgrimage – a coaching journey to wherever they felt God was calling them to grow. In a private, confidential setting, I would be their coach so they would be able to:

- Achieve greater balance and direction in their lives
- Gain clarity of focus and purpose
- Become more aware of their gifts and strengths and who God was calling them to be
- Celebrate the resurrection of new possibilities and visions for their future

This coaching experience affirmed that we are all "wondrously made" in the image of God and that the "glory of God is a person fully alive." Life in Christ offers us a life of abundant love and joy. God's grace is ever-present to us; we need only open ourselves to receive it. Lent can be a great time to pause, reflect, and transform our lives so that we might live God's great gift of life more abundantly. During Lent, each pilgrim went on a journey to a deeper relationship with God in Jesus Christ.

The Lenten Spiritual Journey coaching program was a gift for me as the coach, and coachees reported that it was a great experience for them as well. Their learning and insights were significant, and met or exceeded the hopes and expectations they had at the beginning of the program. I think the specific time limits and the spiritual focus of the season of Lent helped maintain a level of intensity in the process that kept us working on our initial goals and commitments. At the same time, the flexibility of the program allowed each coachee to seek his or her own goals. This process could also work well as a group coaching experience, especially around the use of spiritual disciplines and practices of prayer that could be explored by a group, with the experience shared by all.

~~~~~~~~~~~~~~~~~~~~~~~~~
~~~~~~~~~~~~~~~~~~~~~~~~~

Reverend **Nancy M. DeStefano** is an ordained elder in the United Methodist Church, currently serving at Blue Mound United Methodist Church in Denton, Texas. She is also a licensed clinical social worker in the state of Texas. She holds a certificate in spiritual direction and is currently seeking credentialing as a coach through the International Coach Federation (ICF). She also leads retreats, workshops, and studies on a variety of topics, including a workshop and coaching experience about sage-ing – the concept of moving into the second phase of life mindfully and meaningfully, particularly suited for baby boomers planning for retirement and those already in retirement. Prior to answering the call to ordained ministry, Reverend DeStefano was a therapist/counselor and a high school history teacher. She can be reached at ndestef1@aol.com.

Pickin' That Carcass Clean: Coaching a Congregation through Conflict

By *Patricia K. Suggs*

"Honey, you really picked that carcass clean," said a small, wise, elderly woman. For a coach who works with conflict situations in congregations, this was a wonderful compliment. I was at a small African-American church in a rural area, for the purpose of helping the congregation work through conflict and bond as a community. There was a small group who had been controlling the congregation for a long time, but they now had a pastor who was not allowing that. As a result, their conflicts had been getting worse and more intense.

The following are key points when working in conflict situations:

- Listen to understand
- Speak the truth in love
- Do not make assumptions
- Work towards collaboration

The Coaching4Clergy Five-Step Coaching Model, developed by J. Val Hastings, is a coaching framework that pulls together critical coaching skills. This model blends beautifully with the key concepts of conflict work. In the first part of the model, listening and evoking set the foundation for a trusting relationship. Listening involves words, body language, tone, inflection, rate, and pitch, with no judgment. In the step of evoking, the coach prompts the coachee to say more. The tasks of clarifying and brainstorming provide the pillars for the foundation; the coach must clarify and make sure that he or she is hearing the coachee correctly, while brainstorming is the point at which the coach and the coachee go deeper.

These are the means by which the coach helps the coachee look deep within to find clues and/or answers. The coach then supports the coachee by helping him or her come up with an action plan. This plan helps the coachee move from where they are to where they want to be.

Let's get back to the church and their conflict. We began the intervention with an educational session about the importance of positive communication – speaking and listening in love – and the absence of bullying, triangulation, and gossip. I described the five models of responding to conflict: avoidance, accommodation, competition, compromise, and collaboration.

Our next step was to guide the group in developing a covenant that would explain how they believed people should relate to one another in the church. We started this task with a circle process. Everyone was seated in a circle and each person had the opportunity to speak, describing their experiences in this church – both positive and negative, and giving their perception of what was currently happening in the church. As we went around the circle, it became evident that people were not comfortable with speaking their minds. I emphasized that this was a safe environment, and reminded them of the covenant we had developed.

There was one man who stood out as a respected leader in the church. He was also part of the small group who had been seeking to regain control in the church. Being a coach, I began to ask this gentleman powerful questions. Like peeling the layers of an onion, slowly we went deeper and deeper. With each question, he became more and more willing to share. The information he shared turned out to be very important for the church in beginning to move further. After he spoke, other members began to open up and share. At one point, one person from the small group got up and left, and this action spoke volumes to the rest of the group.

It took several questions per person to get to the deeper truth, but several sessions later we had collected vital information. We discussed the main issues that needed to be addressed and then developed strategies to deal with them. Upon ending the process, the group had developed a stronger bond and a desire to move their church forward in the direction they believed God wanted them to go. While I cannot control how they will use their newfound knowledge and strategies, I know that I helped them look deeper within and discover ways to work more effectively with one another. My prayers are with them as they strive to be the true church.

Most of the churches I go into as a facilitator for conflict are facing similar issues: small groups trying to control the church, people who are always negative, and people who are power-hungry. Having coaching skills in my toolbox has enhanced my ability to work with any and all of the situations I face. Coaching encourages openness and careful listening, helping people go deeper within themselves to solve issues, and being encouraging and supportive even in the midst of disagreement.

Coaching has a valuable place in ministry. Whether we are working in churches as pastors or lay leaders, or conducting interventions for conflict-ridden congregations, coaching can make a powerful difference. After all, life is about community, about relationships, about truly being with other people.

In another example of a conflict situation, I found a church in which the congregation was divided. The pastor had been withdrawn from leadership, and the church was truly suffering, unsure of their future and how they would ever come together again. As I stood to give my first sermon, I could feel the pain and unhappiness, and sense the loss of energy. Thus began my two years of interim ministry. My first job was to love and nurture them. With a great deal of careful listening, I was able to discover the deep hurts. Asking powerful questions that engaged the members in constructive discussions about their future allowed them to gain back their confidence and look to the future in a positive way.

In conflict work, coaching is invaluable. The goal is twofold: listen to the members and present them with probing questions, and then train them to do the same. How often do we have the opportunity to really share our stories? During this intervention each person shares his or her story while everyone else practices listening to hear the whole story – what is said and un-said. A trained coach can then help pull out the relevant details.

Coaching is also valuable when working with an administrative board struggling to discover its church's vision. Using listening skills, intuition, and powerful questions, you can uncover any barriers to the church's ability to achieve their vision. You may also discover that sometimes people say they want growth, but what they really want is new people who are just like them. They're not really willing to step out in faith and grow in the way and direction in which God wants them to grow. Only deep conversations can uncover these issues, when people are lovingly confronted with questions that cause them to look below the surface issues.

Thus, coaching can be used in many areas in parish ministry including committee meetings, enhancing communication between committees, and vision development work. Coaching allows the committee members to use their creativity – to ask themselves deeper questions and come up with answers instead of depending on the pastor to decide what needs to be done.

The following is wonderful advice for clergy and congregations:

- If you do not go after what you want, you'll never have it.
- If you do not ask, the answer will always be no.
- If you do not step forward, you'll always be in the same place.

Coaching gives you the courage to go after what you want and ask for what you want and need. Coaching enables you to take that step forward and continue on your life's journey more confident, content, and carefree.

I once read a statement that summarizes what the coaching relationship can be. It said, "I'm a strong person. But every now and then I would like someone to take my hand and say everything will be alright." A coach can be your advocate and your encourager, and can help you realize the potential you have to be alright.

"Pickin' that carcass clean" – what a great way to say that we have gone to the deeper levels and discovered the truth(s). Conflicts are very difficult and sensitive situations. Safety, trust, confidence, and willingness to risk are keys in dealing with relationship situations, and especially with conflicts. Wherever there is anger, hurt, or betrayal, coaching is a valuable intervention.

~~~~~~~~~~~~~~~~~~~~~~~~~~
~~~~~~~~~~~~~~~~~~~~~~~~~~

Rev. Dr. Patricia K. Suggs is passionate about helping others develop into the people they were meant to be. She is an ordained elder and endorsed coach in the United Methodist Church. Dr. Suggs is a popular speaker and trainer. Her Master of Divinity degree is from Duke University, and her Ph.D. (in family relations with a special focus in social gerontology) is from the University of North Carolina at Greensboro. She is a certified coach with the International Coach Federation and a faculty member and trainer at Coaching4Clergy. She is also a certified spiritual director and a certified healing touch practitioner, and integrates these modalities in her coaching practice, Coaching Church Leaders, LLC. Her coaching services include working with individuals and groups, as well as leading congregations and other groups through conflict and reconciliation. She offers training (seminars, workshops, and teleclasses) in the following areas: leadership development, team development, conflict/reconciliation, coaching, and spiritual formation. For more information, visit www.coachingchurchleaders.com, email pksuggs@coachingchurchleaders.com, or call 336-918-2974.

Breaking the Silence: Using Coaching at the End of Life

By *Don Eisenhauer*

It was nearing 5:00 pm. I couldn't wait to go home, eat dinner, and relax.

Just then the phone rang. "Dad has taken a turn for the worse. We think he is dying. The whole family is here. We could really use you. Would you mind coming by?"

When I arrived at John's home, I was ushered to his bedroom where he was in bed, totally unresponsive. His breathing was labored and he was gurgling loudly (what some call "the death rattle"). His mouth was wide open, in the shape of an O. There were fifteen family members in the room, encircling the bed, both adults and children. Some were crying hysterically. Some had blank looks on their faces. Some were teary and were quietly wiping their eyes. No one said a word. Every eye was focused on me. They stared, waiting for me to speak.

Variations of this true story are experienced by most pastors, church leaders, coaches, hospice chaplains, military chaplains, and others in ministry. People in our culture are uneasy with end-of-life issues, and many have never talked or even thought about their own death or about grieving the loss of a loved one. When they find themselves face to face with this issue – as did the family in my story – they have no clue how to respond and they desperately look for help. Their pastor/chaplain/church leader is often the one to whom they turn.

What are the needs of this dying man? How about his grieving family?

Most do not need a counselor to fix them or help them get over the emotions they are experiencing. Most do not need a therapist to make them feel better at the moment. Rarely do they need a theologian to come and correct their theology. Rather, through deep listening and powerful questions, someone who understands the principles of end-of-life coaching can walk this journey with them. He or she will help them embrace what is happening in them and around them, and seek God's transformation in the midst of it.

I am convinced that in most cases people have within them everything they need to deal with the inevitable end-of-life issues. For many reasons, however, most are not aware of how to tap those resources. We need someone to come alongside of us and help bring out the potential within. When we feel like we are going crazy, we need to be reminded that we are normal. When we feel empty and alone, we need to be supported. When we feel angry and are ready to explode, we need someone who will allow us to be real. When it seems too difficult to go on, we need to be encouraged. When our story begs to be told, we need someone to listen. And when we feel hopeless and want to give up, we need someone to help us form a new vision for the future. The end-of-life coach helps people do these things.

Using end-of-life coaching skills with John and his family would include addressing the following issues:

- The pastor's/coach's own views about dying, death, and grief. Before one can effectively minister to another at the end of life, he or she must process past deaths within their own family and friendships, evaluate their feelings concerning the fact that they will one day die, and make sure they are effectively mourning past losses in their own life.
- The way our world (and the church) deals with (or does NOT deal with) end-of-life issues. What John and his family have learned and been exposed to will affect how they respond in this situation.
- The normal process of death. The pastor/coach who wants to minister to those at the end of life should be aware of what happens to the human body as it begins to shut down and die. Most have not watched someone die, and therefore do not know what to expect.

- What happens to an individual after death? Is there life after death? If so, how does one get there? Even those who have not been interested in spiritual things all through their lives usually become interested when they know they are dying.
- The needs of the dying. What should one say – or not say – to the dying? Are there helpful things to talk about before one dies? What is necessary for a peaceful death?
- Normal grief. How should one respond after a loved one dies? How does one mourn well? The pastor/coach should be aware that in spite of what is or is not culturally acceptable, mourning is necessary.
- Practical issues. These may include funeral plans and writing a will, a living will, and/or an ethical will.
- The role of children in end-of-life issues. Should they be there? A pastor/coach can help children process death and learn how to grieve. Many parents are confused about this issue.
- Ongoing follow-up. A plan must be in place for implementing and managing follow-up with the family of the deceased.

Let's go back to my visit at John's bedside. I broke the silence, acknowledging that this was a difficult, emotional time, and that it was okay for those gathered to express their feelings. As the tears flowed, I affirmed them in the release of their emotions, and spoke of the value of tears. I reminded the male family members (who appeared embarrassed by their emotions) that real men do cry.

When they were ready to listen, I told the family that John appeared to be comfortable, and explained that his gurgling was normal and not painful to him, even though it was painful for them to hear. I invited them to share what the day in John's bedroom had been like. For quite a while family members took turns sharing their stories – their perspectives of what was occurring and how it affected them. I affirmed them in their sharing and said, "Tell me more," "How did that make you feel?" and "Thank you for sharing." I asked if there were other family members who might want to come see John before he died.

I reminded the family that even though this time in John's bedroom was difficult, it was also a great privilege. Many never get the opportunity to say the things they want to say to their loved ones before they die. I encouraged the family not to miss that opportunity with John. I gave them some examples of helpful things to share.

I specifically asked the children what it was like for them to see their grandfather like this. I asked them to share their memories of John, and reminded them that those memories were theirs to hold on to forever; no one could take them away. I listened as the children shared, I affirmed their presence there, and I answered their questions. They wanted to know what was happening to John's body and what would happen to him after he died. Based on John's Christian faith, I explained how wonderful heaven would be, and that they could know that John would be there. I talked with them about the funeral service (which the family had already preplanned with John's input) and prepared them for what it would be like.

I listened as the whole family reminisced, shared their love with John, and told him goodbye.

I asked the family if they would like me to pray for John and for them. Then they joined hands with each other, including John and me, and I prayed for a comfortable, peaceful death for John, and for God's perfect timing. I prayed for comfort for the family, for a clear sense of God's presence, and for the family to support each other through this time. I gave thanks for heaven, and for the hope of eternal life. I prayed for wisdom in knowing the best ways to continue to support and minister to this family through this time of loss.

Even though it had been a long day, I felt energized by my time with John's family. John was still unresponsive, but the family was no longer silent. They were talking to John, sharing the things dear to their hearts. They were supporting each other, sharing memories, and openly expressing their feelings. They were beginning to grieve appropriately, and to mourn the loss of a man who would be greatly missed. As I prepared to leave, there was a wonderful sense of peace and God's presence.

No one in John's bedroom needed to be fixed. They didn't need me to help them feel better or correct their thinking or beliefs. They simply needed me to coach them – to meet them right where they were and walk their journey with them.

I will continue to support John's family through their time of grief. I will stay in touch with them, listen to their stories, provide helpful resources, and let them know that they are not forgotten.

I know of no greater privilege than coaching at the end of life and walking this journey with others.

~~~~~~~~~~~~~~~~~~~~~~~~~~~~

Dr. Don Eisenhauer, ACC, is a pastor and an associate certified coach who is currently serving as a hospice chaplain and bereavement coordinator. He co-authored the book *Coaching at End of Life: A Coach Approach to Ministering to the Dying and the Grieving*, and trains pastors on this topic. He is also the co-founder of the Bereavement Management Group, providing software to help in the care of the grieving. You can learn more about this program at www.bereavementmanagement.com.
~~~~~~~~~~~~~~~~~~~~~~~~~~~~

Ephesians 4:11-13

It was he who gave some to be pastors . . . to prepare God's people for works of service so that the body of Christ may be built up until we all reach unity in the faith and in knowledge of the Son of God and become mature, attaining to the whole measure of the fullness of Christ.

SECTION TWO

Leadership and Team Development

In this extraordinary time, as the ministry platelets change and shift, leadership is what's needed. Actually, *outstanding* leadership is what's needed.

Years ago I heard someone say, "Great leaders are born!" Nothing could be further from the truth. Yes, we're born with unique traits and temperaments that may or may not lend themselves to leadership. But the reality is that great leaders are developed and empowered. And coaching skills are a key part of that developmental process.

Take me, for example. After completing the StrengthsFinder assessment, I remember being disappointed about learning that "Woo" wasn't one of my top strength themes. I immediately thought, how can I lead a global movement without "Woo"? The coaches I have worked with over the years knew differently, and helped me understand and appreciate that I was exactly what was needed for this global movement – even without "Woo."

(Incidentally, my top strength themes are: Strategic, Futurist, Maximizer, Activator, and Achiever. A friend, commenting on my themes, remarked, "With those strengths you are a force to be reckoned with." I think he might be right.)

This section contains examples of how coaches develop an individual or a team. Imagine that development of high-capacity leadership were the norm in ministry. Wow! What a difference.

After the Honeymoon: Coaching a Ministry Supervisor

By J. Val Hastings

For the past twenty-eight years Mark had been a very successful and effective pastor. The three churches that he pastored all grew exponentially. Mark was one of those individuals who inspire others. Leadership came naturally to him, as did vision casting.

Mark had been promoted to a supervisory role in his denomination, and was now supervising over ninety pastors and churches. He was just beginning his third year in this new role when he first connected with me.

The first two years had gone well, similar to the "honeymoon times" he had experienced in the churches he pastored. Now the honeymoon was over. In past leadership roles, his third year was when momentum really began to swell and grow. Typically, in the past, the honeymoon transitioned into a major growth spurt, followed by a new vision of ministry.

None of this was happening in Mark's new supervisory role, and he was beginning to question whether he was right for this role. He had even begun exploring other positions, such as going back to being the lead pastor at a local church. His supervisor and advisory board wanted him to stay and were trying their best to encourage him.

Mark had attended the required supervisory training that his denomination had developed for new supervisors. This included an annual weekend retreat with other new supervisors, when he would also be paired with a mentoring supervisor. These events often digressed to denominational business, which only served to further frustrate Mark.

He had looked for solutions by reading the latest ministry leadership books, and even tried what they recommended. Yet nothing really changed.

Mark subscribed to the Coaching4Clergy monthly newsletter and my blog. He emailed me with the feedback that he found my articles to be more helpful than the latest leadership books. After several email exchanges, he asked for a complimentary coaching session, and then hired me as his coach.

My ideal coachee is someone who is really, really ready for something new and different. That was definitely Mark. He was eager to be coached and equally keen to do the follow-up work. Early on in our coaching, we surfaced several limiting beliefs Mark had about himself, his role, and his denomination.

One of these limiting beliefs was that he couldn't really be himself in his supervisory role. Mark had always been an independent thinker, unafraid to challenge an individual or group. At denominational gatherings he often spoke candidly about unpopular issues. Yet he described his new role as having to be "the company guy." Upon further exploration, Mark recalled that his bishop had asked him to take this role specifically because he *wasn't* a "company guy." This awareness alone gave Mark a tremendous newfound freedom, and his passion and energy returned.

Once Mark uncovered his "company guy" limiting belief, our subsequent coaching sessions focused on other limiting beliefs and getting to the core of what was at hand. His leadership effectiveness increased. Pastors began requesting to be placed under Mark's supervision. He asked for a second term in his role as supervisor, and this was granted – an honor that is almost unheard of.

In addition to coaching, Mark has also received coach training. While he has limited opportunities to coach the pastors that he supervises, his goal is to make his newfound coaching skills available to all of the pastors and churches within his reach.

Over the years I have had numerous opportunities to provide coaching and coach training to supervisory and conference-level leaders like Mark, and I would like to take this opportunity to offer a couple of personal comments and observations:

- I applaud leaders like Mark who seek outside or additional help that will further hone and perfect their own leadership skills. The shift from leadership in a local church to a supervisory, conference-level leadership role is a dramatic one. Often, as with Mark, limiting beliefs surface and get in the way.
- Now, more than ever, we are in need of outstanding, effective leaders. The ministry platelets are shifting and there is seismic evidence all around us. Mediocre, play-it-safe leadership is not acceptable! I want to personally invite supervisors and conference leaders to follow in Mark's footsteps – continue to create coaching and coach training opportunities for those you supervise while also taking advantage of those same services yourself. You will all benefit. We need you to be at the top of your game!

Effective leadership is not a luxury, but a necessity.

~~~~~~~~~~~~~~~~~~~~~~~~~

J. Val Hastings, MCC, is the founder and president of Coaching4Clergy, which provides specialized training for pastors, church leaders, and coaches. Val hired his first coach while he was pastoring at a local United Methodist church. His progress was noticed by all, and he began to wonder, "What if I adopted a coaching approach to ministry? What if the larger church adopted a coaching approach to ministry?" In that moment a vision began to emerge – a global vision: *Every pastor, ministry staff, and church leader a coach.*

Val is the author of *The Next Great Awakening: How to Empower God's People with a Coach Approach to Ministry,* and the e-book *The E3-Church: Empowered, Effective and Entrepreneurial Leadership That Will Keep Your Church Alive.* Val currently holds the designation of master certified coach through the International Coach Federation, the highest coaching designation.
~~~~~~~~~~~~~~~~~~~~~~~~~

Transforming Good Pastors into Great Pastors: The Leadership Development Group Coaching Project

By Larry Ousley

"The Glory of God is a human being fully alive." – St. Irenaeus, 2nd century

"Larry, I've decided you are right – coaching is the best way to help pastors and churches accomplish their missions!" It was ironic that my friend the Reverend Kelvin Sauls was calling me while I was attending an advanced coach training event for Path One coaches. Path One coaches work with pastors of new church starts within the United Methodist Church (UMC). Kelvin began to talk with me about a potential pilot coaching project that could be replicated across the denomination.

Kelvin was the director of congregational development for the General Board of Global Ministries (GBGM) of the UMC. Also, he had particular responsibilities for revitalizing ethnic minority churches in the United States. He had participated in Covenant Coaching Circles (CCC), a program that I created with the help and leadership of my coaching colleague, Dr. Jim Robey. Through CCC, Kelvin experienced both the power and potential of group coaching. Now he was encouraging me to work with an annual conference or some other regional body to use coaching as part of a larger project of congregational development with ethnic minority pastors and churches. He suggested that GBGM's matching grant program might help fund it.

Kelvin and I felt that although I had done a lot of work with race relations, since I am Caucasian it would be best if I partnered with a person with an ethnic heritage. I immediately thought of my colleague Dr. Carl Arrington, who was the director of African-American ministries for the Southeast Jurisdiction (SEJ) of the UMC. Carl and I had worked together on other projects and he had been a participant in the first CCC group, where he'd received some coach training.

Carl and I began to explore the idea of a coaching project with several annual conferences within the UMC. Eventually we created the Leadership Development Group Coaching Project with the South Carolina (SC) Conference. We had coordinating assistance from Dr. Ken Nelson, Director of African-American Ministries for the SC Conference, as well as support from Ken's supervisor, the Reverend Willie Teague, Director of Connectional Ministries, and Bishop Mary Virginia Taylor and her cabinet as a whole. Ken applied for and received a grant of $15,000 from GBGM, which was matched by the conference. Each participant paid $100 and covered their transportation to the two retreats and the long distance charges for the group coaching calls.

Together, Carl, Ken, and I agreed on ten outcomes for the ten-month project, which would combine group coaching, individual coaching, and retreats. We did some pre-project assessment around the ten outcomes to have a baseline for the effectiveness of our work together.

Outcomes

The pastors will:

1. partner with the congregation to develop a shared vision of ministry.
2. learn how to build a staff using a team approach, or develop a team approach with existing staff.
3. increase worship attendance by 5 percent.
4. increase financial giving by 5 percent.
5. create a written plan for lay leadership development that encourages people to serve in the area of their gifts.

6. develop one or two new ministries (e.g. small groups, discipleship ministries, or Bible study).

7. establish a personal plan for continuing education that will support their spiritual growth and the development of skills needed to implement the vision.

8. establish and be accountable for self-care goals.

9. establish and be accountable for spirituality goals.

10. select a ministry tool or strategy (based on the vision) that will help the congregation and pastor take the next step in ministry (e.g. Natural Church Development (NCD), Five Practices of Fruitful Congregations, coaching). Clergy are to provide written documentation of the selected tool.

All of the ten pastors and churches who participated in the ten-month program had increases in all ten outcomes, except for one pastor with extenuating circumstances. Even that pastor had improvements in scoring in most of the areas.

Process

Group coaching

The heart of our program was group coaching. Twice per month we met by telephone conference for seventy-five minutes using the powerful, interactive platform, Maestro Conference. Each session focused on a particular aspect of the outcomes. In addition, during each session we focused on the participants' accountability for their self-care and spiritual goals. Initially Carl and I led the coaching around this, and then as we taught the participants basic coaching skills we had them coach each other.

Individual coaching

Another key aspect of the project was individual coaching. Carl and I divided the group randomly, and each of us coached five pastors once per month throughout the ten months, for about thirty minutes per session. This allowed us to meet each pastor's individual needs in a confidential setting, which was a significant component of the overall program. In this way we were able to deal with challenges or issues that they might not have felt comfortable sharing in the group coaching sessions.

Retreats

My own experience with virtual coach training has shown me that it is not really necessary to have in-person meetings in order to create intimacy and strong connections as a group. However, the participants and potential participants in these church settings seemed to feel that meeting face-to-face was an important aspect of creating community. Therefore, we included two retreats to help with bonding and to jump-start learning and community building.

We began the whole program with a one-day retreat in Columbia, South Carolina, in August of 2010. It was a central location that allowed the pastors to attend and return home in the evening. We got to know each other, created connections, dealt with expectations and hopes for the project, focused specifically on self-care and spirituality goals, provided an overview of the project, and responded to comments and questions.

Mid-way through the year we had a second retreat, this time a three-day retreat at the Lake Junaluska Conference and Retreat Center at Lake Junaluska, North Carolina. We delved into some content from the ten outcomes that we had not yet covered in our bi-monthly group coaching calls. We gave each participant a role in leading some aspect of this retreat, whether it was a worship session or a workshop about one of the content areas. The group enjoyed being together and deepened their learning and intentionality around their action plans.

Testimonies

Here are a few comments from the participants that were published in the *South Carolina United Methodist Advocate*, March 23, 2011:

- One pastor said that the coaching project has been an invaluable tool for her. "This coaching initiative is good for the conference in that it transforms good pastors into great pastors," she said. "Conference gatherings and district gatherings are valuable tools for fellowship, but coaching takes it to a higher level. Someone once said, 'In order to receive something different, you have to do something different.' We can't afford to keep doing the same old things in our churches and expect different results."

- Another pastor said that the experience has helped him approach ministry and life in new ways. "Too often we as clergy find ourselves not connected with a support group beyond our friends, when our connection has so much to offer," he said. "It opens up a network that is without bias and competition, and for its duration it will bring about community."
- Another person said the program has been a great opportunity for her and the other participants. "Our annual conference is to be commended for this new paradigm in leadership development," she said. "We have been called from different districts, different experiences, and different perspectives to the table of ministry commonality. From my view, this program will continue to speak life to us and blow breath into us as we serve God and God's people for such a time as this."
- In reflecting on the program, Dr. Ken Nelson stated: "I believe that three of the most significant encumbrances to effective, vital congregations are ineffective leadership, a lack of vision, and a lack of partnership between the laity and clergy. The coaching initiative addresses all three of these factors in very specific ways, and builds upon the strengths that these pastors already possess."

Evaluation

We conducted an extensive evaluation at the end of the ten-month project, comparing results with our pre-project assessment of the ten outcomes. All aspects of the initiative met or exceeded our goals. The average increase in worship attendance for the ten churches as a whole was 12.06 percent, which exceeded our goal of 5 percent. Financial giving increased an average of 5.2 percent compared to our goal of 5 percent. The latter is significant in that the timeframe of the project was August 2010 through May 2011 during the height of the economic challenges in our country, which were generally thought to be more severe among African-American persons and thus their churches.

Further, the churches began an average of 2.5 new ministries during the project, compared to our goal of one or two new ministries for each church. Participants learned and incorporated an average of 2.9 new ministry tools into their ministry. Pastors rated their overall experience as 9.7 out of 10.

Learnings and Reflections

- Multiple means of coaching and learning (group and individual coaching as well as in-person retreats) allowed participants to experience the unique benefits of each modality, and is the ideal structure for this type of program. In our case, this was possible due to our luxurious budget of $31,000 – $15,000 each from GBGM and the SC Conference, plus $100 each from the ten participants.
- However, group coaching is the most cost-effective coaching method. While we had other components in this program, the group sessions provided *laser coaching* for each individual and enabled ongoing connection, accountability, and transformation as part of a learning community. Studies show that the more people to whom one is accountable, the better the follow-through. Therefore, sharing one's commitments in a group setting raises the bar above that kind of accountability with one's own coach. Further, as Fred Craddock has said, "we overhear better than we hear." Thus, we can sometimes gain insights by listening to others being coached in the group setting. This observation of coaching also allows participants to pick up on coaching skills.
- One of my concerns about coaching in the church is the perceived high expense of coaching. While the evaluation of this project demonstrated the relative value of these multiple means of coaching and learning, they also made the project more expensive. Particular deluxe elements included the two in-person retreats (at no additional cost to the participants), having two coaches working together in all phases of the project, and having individual coaching sessions throughout the ten months. Any or all of these deluxe elements could be omitted or adjusted if financial resources are limited. Here are my feelings about the relative value of the various elements of the initiative:

    - Retreats: The retreats represented about 30 percent of the budget, and I believe they added a 10 percent increase in effectiveness and satisfaction for the participants.

    - Two coaches: Having two coaches involved in every phase of the project probably added about 40 percent to the cost. While it was very helpful initially for me as a Caucasian to have an African-American coach as a partner in order to be accepted by the participants, having two coaches rather than one probably only added 10 percent to the program's effectiveness.

    - Individual coaching: Individual coaching is the most powerful and customizable method of coaching. However, in this project it probably represented about 30 percent of the budget. How much better was the project because the individual coaching was included? This is a difficult question to answer. I believe it added 20 percent to the effectiveness of the program, but that it is perhaps not worth the extra expense if resources are limited.

    - Bottom line: When financial resources are limited, I believe 75 percent of the benefit of this kind of leadership development coaching project could be achieved with 40 percent of the cost by eliminating the retreats and the individual coaching. If you eliminated one of the coaches as well, you might expect 70 percent of the benefits for 20 percent of the cost. Nevertheless, the full multiple means approach was more effective as a whole, although more costly.

- Having measurable and definite outcomes seemed to help everyone get in gear to work to make them happen. If we had been more causal about our goals, my guess is that the coachees would have accomplished less.
- Being in the group throughout the ten-month program had a buoying effect to help lift all the participants toward more excellence, also known as "raising one's game."

Through the Leadership Development Group Coaching Project, the participants, and consequently their churches, were more fully alive in Christ. Consider organizing a group coaching project in your sphere of influence.

~~~~~~~~~~~~~~~~~~~~~~~~~

Dr. Larry Ousley (Larry@LarryOusley.com) is the executive director of the Intentional Growth Center (IGC). Before coming to IGC in 2000, he served as senior pastor of several large churches. He is a professional certified coach (PCC) through the International Coach Federation. Larry is also an endorsed life coach through the United Methodist Endorsing Agency, a certified organizational relationship systems coach (ORSCC) and a faculty member at Coaching4Clergy. You can visit his website at www.LarryOusley.com.
~~~~~~~~~~~~~~~~~~~~~~~~~

Who Can Help? Coaching a Stuck Church Committee

By Jim Latimer

It was the first week of December, and Christmas was fast approaching. The Mission Committee had gathered for an intense planning session for the Gifts for Kids program. They had just one week to get the Christmas tree up in the narthex, tastefully decorated with individual ornament-style tags, each bearing the name of a child in a foster home and his or her wishes for gifts from Santa. They also had to inform the congregation about how to participate.

Susan (Committee Chair): "I contacted Rainbow Children's Home for the list of children's names again this year, but had trouble getting connected to the right person. Bill, the man who has coordinated this with me in the past, is no longer there, and the woman who answered the phone didn't know who took his place. She was familiar with the program and was sure they'd want to receive our gifts again this year. She said she'll find out and call me back."

Barb: "So what can we do in the meantime?"

Susan: "We have to get the tree set up, get the instructions out, set up a table, and book someone to attend it at both services for the next two Sundays. Who can help?"

Brittany: "I'll contact Jack to get the tree out of the attic."

Susan: "We need to get the word out to the congregation quickly. Who can contact the church secretary to get notices put in the church bulletin and on the website and where else? (silence…)

"By the way, has anyone seen Jenny or Linda? They're part of this committee but haven't come to a meeting in quite a while. Does anyone know why? Are they still interested?"

"Beth or Corrine, would you be willing to do this?"

Beth: "I'd be willing to do it again this year but it takes a lot of time and my mother is sick and I just can't spare the time."

Susan: "Corrine, how about you?"

Corrine: "I've never done it before. I'm willing to try if no one else will. But my husband is still upset with me for spending so much time coordinating our charity event a couple months ago."

Susan: (sigh…) "Yes, I know what you mean. My family is also wondering why I spend so much time on Mission Committee things. They think it's a good cause, but not enough to participate themselves."

The church had been participating in the Gifts for Kids program at Christmastime for who knows how long, though year after year there had been fewer gifts donated and delivered. The committee worked hard behind the scenes so the congregation could participate. The drill was the same every time: Contact the foster home, get the names of all the kids with their ages, their interests, and what gifts they'd like Santa to bring them. Then set up the tree, get the tags on it, publicize and promote the program, coordinate the deliveries, and more. The program still seemed like a good idea, but it was always a big relief for the committee when the gifts were finally all delivered. It's a lot of work.

Committee members love their church! They are women of faith. (No one can remember the last time a man was part of this committee.) They are all mothers or grandmothers with families. Many have grown children. They are natural caregivers with hearts drawn to those who need love, a meal, or a hug, or even a gift from Santa at Christmas.

As pastor, I was fairly new to the church. I had recently been through coaching training and was looking for ways to apply what I'd learned. The Mission Committee seemed a good candidate for a coaching approach. Susan and I hit it off from the start. She's a natural leader with a compassionate heart and a desire to see her church move forward.

"Hi Susan. How's the Mission Committee going?" I asked.

"Oh, it's okay," she sighed, "but it feels like 'same old same old.'"

"What do you mean?" I asked.

"We just keep doing the same things. It's pretty boring."

"It sounds like folks may be ready for a fresh approach." I replied. "Would it be okay if I come to your next meeting to facilitate a discussion around the committee's work and purpose?"

"Sure!" she replied.

For as long as anyone could remember, the Mission Committee had been devoted to organizing various opportunities for church members to participate in charitable giving. No one was arguing that charitable giving was unimportant. The problem was this: Most of the committee members were on the verge of burning out or wishing they were somewhere else. So after initial remarks by Susan and me about the purpose of my joining their meeting, I asked them, "How's it going?"

They responded with eye rolls, shrugged shoulders, and details of past charity events.

"I'm not hearing much excitement or passion. Let me ask this: What do *you* want to do?" A long silence followed.

Beth asked, "What do you mean, 'What do *we* want to do?' We're here to serve the church! Aren't we supposed to do what the *church* wants us to do?"

However, we all knew they were stuck, so I pressed on: "You have the right to get something out of this, too. What kind of mission activities would *you* get excited about participating in?"

The reply was quick, "We'd like to do more hands-on things. We want to meet the people we're helping and hear their stories. We want to connect with them personally."

"Then why don't you?" I responded.

More silence.

"May I share an idea with you?" I asked. "Sure," they replied.

"This brochure from Family Hope came to my mailbox last month. Look it over and let me know what you think."

At their next meeting they were more energized than usual. "The energy among you seems quite different than last time. What's happening?" I asked.

"We called Family Hope for more information. We really like what we hear!" Susan said. "Rather than splitting up the men and women – a typical practice at homeless shelters that puts an additional strain on intact families – Family Hope client families are housed in local churches. Participating churches host two families a week three times a year. This means we'd really get to connect with them person to person!"

Corrine added, "At first, having homeless families staying in our church seemed like a crazy idea. We've never done anything like that before. But we love the direct contact we'd have with the families as we share meals and social time with them," she continued. "The Family Hope executive director is coming to meet with us next Sunday morning!"

Before long, the congregation voted to participate in this rich, hands-on hospitality ministry. Soon thirty members of the congregation became actively involved and enthusiastic – nearly one quarter of the congregation.

What I Learned from Coaching This Committee

Looking back, it seemed so easy: Just ask a few good questions, and presto – they get unstuck and the passion for ministry flows again! Certainly the questions helped, but they were effective because of other factors.

First, this committee was ready to be coached. There was enough pain to risk questioning the status quo and limiting assumptions, yet still enough commitment and flexibility to entertain questions and change.

Second, the Mission Committee had a leader who understood the coaching approach and enthusiastically embraced it.

Third, she was respected by her fellow committee members. Since most the work of coaching happens between coaching sessions, local leadership is essential in keeping the ball rolling. Furthermore, without an effective leader on the committee, as a newer coach who was also part of the larger system (as pastor) I could have been tempted to take on this role myself. This would have compromised my objective position as coach.

Fourth, I had permission to coach. By getting Susan's buy-in for me to "facilitate a discussion around the committee's work and purpose," she was able to introduce my presence at that first meeting and endorse my purpose. This enabled others to engage.

Fifth, I had patience. A coaching approach is foreign to folks who are used to carrying out the agendas of others. It may take several meetings, or not pan out at all. Don't force it. In this case, the initial session got the ball rolling, but I had several more with them for accountability, support, and follow-up.

Last, I checked in with the leader between sessions. Susan had put herself on the line with our coaching work and was the key force guiding its new direction. My weekly phone calls to listen and offer support helped her confidently lead the committee into new waters.

~~~~~~~~~~~~~~~~~~~~~~~~~

Rev. James H. Latimer, ACC, works with resourceful, creative church leaders and groups leading intentional revitalization efforts. He helps them get a strong start and continue to a strong finish by defining expectations, orchestrating successes, and overcoming challenges. Jim is an International Coach Federation (ICF) certified coach and is ordained in the United Church of Christ. He holds degrees from Cornell University, Georgia Tech, and the Pacific School of Religion. He is the founder of www.strongstartcoaching.com and serves on the faculty of Coaching4Clergy.
~~~~~~~~~~~~~~~~~~~~~~~~~

From Fragile to Fruitful: How Coaching Assisted a Pastor with a Struggling Church

By Ed George

In the midst of churches marked by divisions, open conflict, mistrust, disillusionment, and failure of mission, pastoring is challenging work at best and downright painful at worst. Serving as a pastor means you continually have the opportunity to discover unique situations and face new challenges. Consequently, you have opportunities to try new things. This brings equal amounts of excitement and concern.

For example, a coachee of mine found herself in a challenging situation when she accepted a role as interim pastor at a metropolitan church in the southwestern US. Diane had more than thirty years' experience in the clergy, but she quickly recognized that she needed help with her temporary placement. And Diane was not a pastor who had one year of experience thirty times; rather, she had thirty years of consecutive ministry experience as a pastor and district superintendent. She was a powerful woman in her own right – a bright, articulate, passionate, well-read, and creative leader and manager. And she also happened to be very wise.

The previous pastor had left the church due to a crisis of faith, and another employee was released due to allegations of misappropriation of funds. Diane was tasked with helping the church become functional and healthy, while preparing it for a permanent pastor. Did I mention that Diane is courageous and faith-filled?

Fragile to Fruitful Bonds

Diane and I worked together for about nine months, preparing the way for a permanent pastor. The task was not easy, and took a considerable engagement of time, energy, prayer, passion, thought, tears, emotional intelligence, and strategic planning on Diane's part.

The first steps on the journey to bringing health to the congregation had little to do with the congregation or what had previously gone on at the church. Rather, they were the steps to building trust between Diane and me – not in terms of keeping confidences and maintaining confidentiality, but whether Diane could trust *herself* with and to me. Would and could I be a safe place where she could be vulnerable and open, revealing her pain, full range of emotions, hopes and dreams, successes, missteps, assumptions, and expectations without fear of judgment, shaming, or rebuke? That is the question she had to answer, and that every potential coachee has to answer. Thankfully, Diane was able to answer affirmatively for herself, as she found me worthy of her trust. We were able to build on that foundation, creating a strong working relationship based on trust, mutual respect, honesty, and hard questions.

The Minefield

As Diane and I reviewed the church's history and the various dynamics and systems at play within the congregation, several things became abundantly clear:

- Severe conflict between two groups existed because one side opted to be empathetic toward the person who lost his position due to misappropriation of funds, while the other side called for him to be personally responsible for his action. *
- The Human Resources Committee was bound by confidentiality that precluded sharing information with the congregation about that employee. This created mistrust, anger, resentment, and suspicion, and generally exacerbated the problem.
- The previous pastor's crisis of faith had deeply impacted the church, creating a ripple effect among both ungrounded believers and some established members. It was an identity crisis in the making.

- The church had experienced several losses in recent years, resulting in grief symptoms in several congregants.
- Attempts at consensus had been futile because the most toxic members of the church could not be convinced to participate in consensus through reason, facts, love, or insight.*
- The church's agendas were set by the most dependent and controlling members of the church rather than by the most energetic, visionary, imaginative, and motivated.*
- No one could see how to create win/win situations

*After studying systems theory, especially the writings of Edwin Friedman, I discovered that these issues are quite common in today's highly anxious society. Furthermore, church members respond quite reactively when someone attempts to lead. Leaders beware!

Learning to Dance in the Minefield

Needless to say, Diane did not tackle all of the issues at once. In fact, many of our coaching sessions had little to do with these specific issues or the others that arose during our engagement. Rather, I kept my ear attuned to how well Diane was doing personally and professionally. On the personal level, I kept an eye on her daily habits – getting enough rest, working out at the gym, eating healthy meals, maintaining regular prayer and devotional time, etc. I wanted to make sure she was taking care of herself as well as she was taking care of the church and its problems.

Though Diane had a personal rule that she would not get too emotionally attached or involved, when she started reporting more fatigue than usual it became clear that that rule had been violated. As we explored her frustration with her overinvestment, she was able to find its roots in her family of origin. There, in order to be accepted and valued, she had had to work hard and prove her worth. The lesson stuck, and served her well all during her ministry. But in this situation, the harder she worked and the more she pushed, the more resistance she experienced and the less the progress she made.

So, for Diane, the focus was to work smarter, not harder. The way to work smarter was through focusing on her personhood – her being in Christ. She reported connecting with Christ in a deeper, more profound sense than ever before. Her focused center in Christ served to quiet her soul and still her in the midst of the free-floating anxiety within the church. Diane began to embody what Edwin Friedman calls "self-knowledge" and "self-control," which are the requisites for being a "self-differentiated" leader. Hence, professionally speaking, I kept an ear attuned to Diane's ability to serve as a leader in three related areas, asking the following questions:

Can she remain separate while still remaining connected? (Self-differentiation)

Was she maintaining her integrity in the midst of chaos and craziness? (Calm, absence of anxiety)

Was she able to manage her own reactivity to the automatic reactivity of others? Can she take stands at the risk of displeasing others? (Being present with those she was leading)

During the course of our work, it became clear that Diane became better at managing her anxiety as she encountered each new opportunity to test her new skills and her new ways of being with people. Toward the end of our scheduled calls, I would hear traces of anxiety in her voice, ask her about it, and then coach her regarding what might be going on at that time and how she might regain her center. With insight and wisdom she was able to make the shift and get back on track for the next opportunity. Once a pastor possesses self-awareness and self-control, and has developed the capacity for self-differentiation, it is much easier to learn how to dance in the minefield.

~~~~~~~~~~~~~~~~~~~~~~~~~

Ed George began full-time ministry in 1980, providing pastoral leadership for churches and religious institutions of various sizes in rural and urban settings. In 1988, he began working in healthcare, serving as an Association for Clinical Pastoral Education clinical pastoral education supervisor for twenty-three years. An elder in full connection with the Central Texas Conference (CTC) of The United Methodist Church (UMC), he founded his own coaching firm, EDG Advantage Coaching, LLC, in 2010. Currently George is the facilitator of the Healthy Church Initiative and Cluster Groups at the CTC UMC, a network of more than 300 churches. George provides resources and training to laity, pastors, and leadership. www.edgadvantagecoaching.com
~~~~~~~~~~~~~~~~~~~~~~~~~

Hearing the History of the Heart: Internal Coaching as an Executive Pastor

By C. Darrell Roland

It had been about year since Pastor Craig accepted leadership of a multi-site campus of Reach Church. The year had been filled with a variety of ups and downs, however something was still burning in Craig's heart to lead this congregation to become a stable and growing campus for Reach Church. Prior to Craig, the campus had experienced much leadership turnover, leaving the attendees disillusioned and disappointed. He knew the task was big, yet had no idea of the depth of the responsibility. You see, Craig had been a student pastor for fourteen years prior to accepting this new responsibility. In addition, his role as student pastor remained intact, so this was not only a new role, but an addition to his existing responsibilities.

Because of my role as executive pastor, I knew that Craig had been struggling in leading this campus in a clear direction. One Monday as he was walking through the office, I asked if he had a few moments. We stepped into the conference room and began talking. He shared for a bit about how he just couldn't seem to get a clear picture of where to lead. Sure, he was rich with experience in leading youth, but somehow that didn't seem to translate into effective leadership of these families.

This is when I knew I had to switch my hat from executive pastor and colleague to coach. I began asking Craig some discovery questions, and as I listened with clean ears, I began to hear a potential path for coaching. Since as a coach I did not want to lead him to the path, I allowed these questions to help him identify the path.

Of course, he did not know I was coaching him; he only saw a colleague and friend taking the time to care and listen. Our trusting relationship combined with the discovery questions to form a solid platform for a coaching session. Craig shared the history of his heart during the past year, and I listened for the questions that God wanted me to ask. Some questions came out of what he was saying, some came from what he didn't say, and others came from where the Spirit was nudging. If I'd gotten stuck in a coaching formula, I would have missed the dance of the moment. As coaches, especially incognito coaches, we have to listen for His voice in order to touch the moment.

As Craig and I continued, I asked about who he is in his most successful moments. If you've played baseball or are a baseball fan, you are familiar with the sweet spot on the bat that hitters like. Since I knew Craig understood that metaphor, I asked him about his sweet spot, and over the next several minutes he shared about this. From there, I simply asked him what was keeping him from leading from his sweet spot. For him that was an "aha!" moment. He talked about trying to replicate our lead pastor, yet knowing he could not. He then dreamed a bit about what he felt this campus would look like in his sweet spot. To this day, as the campus continues to move forward, projecting Craig's sweet-spot vision, he often refers back to how this one conversation shifted his vision for his campus.

Now, I'm not going to tell you that the campus has become a tremendous success, because it has not at this moment. We are not even sure if it can recover from the tumultuous path it has been on the past few years, but we do know that Craig has found his way as a leader and pastor, and that is simply to be Pastor Craig.

Seize the Coaching Opportunity

I have found that most of my internal coaching in our church is done as a partner in ministry who shows the willingness to support and come alongside. It is rare that I set a "coaching appointment," yet there are often connection times. As a coach in a ministry setting, I encourage you not to get caught up in the coaching session, but seize the opportunity to coach a colleague or friend toward their desired destination – fulfilling all God has for them.

Here are some additional examples of internal coaching scenarios:

Scenario One – Pastor Doug and the Men's Ministry

Pastor Doug had served as a men's pastor for the last two years. He had to deal with some difficult leaders who were handed over to him by his lead pastor. These men were not only challenging, but even unwilling to submit to Doug's authority. This had taken a toll on this young pastor's ministry and heart. He felt that he had not received the appropriate support from the men and his lead pastor. Recently his lead pastor had asked Doug to step back and allow him to take charge of the men's ministry. Doug felt he had failed, and at the same time felt it was an unavoidable outcome to a preset destination. Now he was struggling with hurt and disappointment, and even a lack of direction in his role.

Recommended Approach

Since we didn't have the foundation of a coaching relationship prior to this situation, I knew it was important to begin by strengthening the trust in our relationship. I accomplished this with much listening and affirmation, as well as by restating confidentiality. This was a sensitive situation that would mold Doug long term, and it needed to be handled with care.

This is when I encourage my coachees to dream a little bit; to dig into their "who" and find out what God has placed in their hearts. Questions came up like, "Doug, when you dreamed of ministry, what kept coming to mind?" and "What are some things that you must have in ministry to keep your heart vibrant for ministry?" The goal was for Doug to discover his "who" of God's creation.

Once he had found himself, so to speak, it was time to guide Doug to define his future; I like to call it painting the future with *your* brush and paint. Once he could see the future and the path to take, our conversation steered towards how to get on the path, with continuing powerful questions to help him fill in the details. Then it was time to support Doug in setting these action steps in motion and designing a clear follow-up plan to keep him pointed forward.

Scenario Two – A New Leader Finds His Footing

Reach Church had been without a worship leader for three years, and had recently brought Jacob on board as their worship and media director. Jacob brought to the ministry vast experience in these areas, as well as experience in multi-site ministry, which is a new direction for Reach Church. As Jacob got into the role, he discovered that the three years without leadership had taken a greater toll than he had realized. He was struggling with where to begin and how to turn the momentum forward.

Recommended Approach

In this scenario, I spent a great deal of time getting to know Jacob. I felt that this was important in helping him acclimate to his role and in building the trust that is so important in a coaching relationship. Unlike the previous story about Pastor Craig, I did let Jacob know that I am a coach, and explained more about what coaching is and is not. I told him I would be happy to support him from an objective standpoint as a coach. Jacob was very open to being coached.

I began by asking questions that would help Jacob identify the most pressing needs for getting the momentum going. We also focused a good bit of time on the vision for worship at Reach Church and what he felt was important to do along the way. At that point, we began talking about what a worship leader at Reach Church looks like and what type of leader Jacob had to become in order to develop those worship leaders.

Over the span of several sessions, in a process that continues as I write this, Jacob has established who he is as a leader, his vision of worship in the context of ministry at Reach Church, and the steps he needs to implement first. He values the role of internal coaching, and this continues to be part of our relationship as colleagues.

What is Internal Coaching?

Internal coaching is when you are a part of the environment in which you are coaching. Self-coaching, family coaching, staff coaching, and organizational coaching are all examples of internal coaching. Internal coaching is done anywhere and anytime that you play a role or can benefit from the outcome.

Internal coaching creates an environment for growth and synergy. When people feel supported, valued, and released to be who God has created them to be, they move from "doing" to "being." No one can sustain an existence of only "doing." Over time we tire, and can even become resentful that no one cares about the "who" in us.

Are You Ready to Be an Internal Coach?

Regardless of your role in your ministry, career, or life, you can be an internal coach. Here are some things to remember and implement in being an internal coach:

Internal coaches are:

- Approachable and authentic
- Listeners and loyal
- Relational and real
- Co-laborers and cheerleaders

Internal coaching sessions are:

- Safe and supportive
- Unique and uplifting
- Individualistic and inclusive
- Coachee-focused and confidential

Your Next Steps

Considering everything you've read up to now, consider these questions and points:

1. Where are you positioned to be an internal coach?

   a. ______________________________

   b. ______________________________

   c. ______________________________

2. Who are your potential coachees?

   a. ______________________________

   b. ______________________________

   c. ______________________________

3. How can you begin building the coaching platform? __________

   ____

   ____

   ____

4. When will you begin? ______________________________

Step out and make a difference in the lives of others by becoming a coach and/or exercising your existing coaching skills. People want your coaching; they need it. And the Kingdom of God will be blessed by it.

~~~~~~~~~~~~~~~~~~~~~~~~~
~~~~~~~~~~~~~~~~~~~~~~~~~

C. Darrell Roland, PCC, CCA, spent twenty years in industrial and corporate environments prior to moving into ministry where he has served the past eleven years as an executive pastor for a growing multi-site church. He became a certified church administrator through the National Association of Church Business Administration (NACBA) and Candler Theological Institute. He completed his coaching studies with CoachU, Inc. and Coaching4Clergy, and he is accredited as a professional certified coach with the International Coach Federation. He serves as faculty at Coaching4Clergy, where he is a trainer, class facilitator, coach, and mentor coach to pastors and ministry leaders.

Darrell is co-founder of Red Pin Ministries where he and his team serve churches in a variety of areas including accounting services, consulting, strategy, vision, and organizational structure.

darrell.roland@Coaching4Clergy.com

Through Christ's Lens: Leading a Staff of Coaches

By Jennifer Williams

Coaching to Increase Team Dynamics

The tension was palpable in the room. We'd been sitting and hashing out this plan for nearly forty-five minutes and had gotten nowhere. The youth pastor was getting heated, the children's minister was about to check out, and as the executive pastor I just wanted a decision made. Finally the room went silent and we looked at our Rutherford campus pastor, Chris, who was also a trained coach. He asked us one simple question, we all paused for a moment, and then a refreshed discussion began with clarity and definition coming within moments.

This experience is how we define coaching in our Vision Team – the executive leadership team. Of our seven members, three are trained coaches and are actively involved in coaching in one way or another, and two others have experienced coaching and frequently email J. Val Hastings of Coaching4Clergy in a pinch. We have used coaching to help us create this amazing and dynamic team, and have brought in a coach on numerous occasions.

As we've strived to live out God's vision at CrossPoint Church, we've noticed that our leadership team relies on coaching for two key factors. First, coaching helps us understand each other better. When we get to those heated moments when "conflict is breeding creativity,"[1] team members try to understand where each other stands. We attempt to ask

[1] The author is grateful to Richard Whorl, Organizational Development Specialist, for coining this phrase.

probing questions that get to the heart of the other team member or help identify the need they are feeling. We have found that identifying the underlying passion and/or issue helps us work together to find a solution. This mutual understanding then leads to the second factor of coaching on a team, which is that coaching diffuses conflict. By asking questions and identifying issues together, we see each other through Christ's lens. We are then able to work toward the vision together rather than so easily silo-ing or going off in our own ministry direction.

Coaching into the Vision

Coaching is vital for our team as we work towards a new vision in 2013. 2011 marked the end of a five-year vision; during that time we replaced two twenty-year staff members and started two new campuses. These changes caused tension and much conflict. Now we sit as a brand new team trying to hash out and discern God's new vision for us and the church. In order to help with the discernment process, we are using secular business books as a springboard for discussions centered on identifying our *hedgehog concept* and *three circles*. In the last three months we've worked through *Good to Great* and *Great by Choice* by Jim Collins. Rather than staying focused entirely on the assigned reading material, we use coaching techniques to help us identify our passion. We ask particular questions around the room that help us almost literally see the vision in our midst. We are finding that coaching allows us the opportunity and freedom to discover without feeling threatened or competitive. As we discover each team member's passions through coaching, we are crafting a vision that uses these strengths and builds upon that solid foundation. The vision that is coming alive is intertwining all the members' passions together. Rather than creating a competitive environment in which youth ministry is fighting worship for ministry funds, our coaching questions ask, "How can youth ministry and worship work together to move the church forward?"

We recently had one of those "aha!" moments in a team discussion centering on the vision at our three different campuses. We were still struggling with the decision about having separate hedgehog concepts for each campus, or one overarching hedgehog for CrossPoint Church. In the middle of one of these discussions we started talking about our youngest and smallest campus and its outreach ministries. This campus is seeing growth and health by ministering to the least, the last, and the lost in several different ways.

When Chris, the Rutherford campus pastor, posed a question to the entire team, we all identified a passion around this campus's outreach efforts. Suddenly ideas started pouring forth from every ministry area about how we could improve this mission campus: children's ministry had a passion for starting a tutoring ministry for underprivileged children; youth ministry wanted to do hands-on mission; worship wanted to add a multi-cultural element with worship songs and prayers; and the other two campuses wanted to deploy other laypeople into mission at this campus. Without asking the right questions and allowing for dialogue and debate, this shared passion might not have come to light. After all, the campus ministry had not changed in four years, and the leadership team at the campus was basically the same; all that had changed was the coaching techniques of our Vision Team in identifying this new CrossPoint-wide vision. Now we had identified what we all can get excited about and what can motivate us *and* the church into the future.

Coaching Laity into Ministry

As a traditional, main-line, denominational church, we have struggled with what it means to be a fast-moving church of the twenty-first century. In the 1980s and 1990s, the pendulum swung away from utilizing our traditional model of boards and committees to a staff-driven environment. However, in the 2000s we found that this model no longer fit. It had become too easy for the congregation to depend upon the staff and see ministry as being done by others. Today we are working towards a model that identifies the passion of every member and deploys them into that ministry area.

This model relies heavily on coaching. In order to find passion and energy, we have to dig deeply by asking the right questions. We see our seven Vision Team members as coaches who walk with people until those people find their ministry niches. This coaching requires building individual relationships, which often takes time. Yet the outcome is increased ownership among the congregation.

We've seen the most successful example of this model of coaching in our food pantry at our Rutherford campus. Chris, the campus pastor, walks with the members of the food pantry team, and yet does not *do* the ministry himself. He sees that his role is to coach this ministry to the greatest heights by using those whom God brings to this area. When the pantry needed to be redesigned, the pantry team identified who had the gift of design, and created a welcoming space. When additional funds were needed, it was the team, not the staff, who looked for a grant writer.

This coaching model also occurs at our South Hanover campus, designed for those who do not like traditional church. Jason, the campus pastor, utilized the laity at that campus to create a coffeehouse that is open daily. By coaching the lay people, the leadership team created a vision of reaching out by selling coffee. Now church members hang out and drink coffee every day, sharing the message of Jesus in a totally new environment. All this began with Jason coaching the leadership team and asking the right questions to ignite passion.

The Preacher as Coach

We very recently identified the next step for coaching at CrossPoint – the Sunday sermon. One of our teaching pastors was struggling with how to preach the scripture in which the soldiers flog Jesus just prior to the crucifixion. It was Lent, and the sermon topics were walking through the traditional Lenten texts, yet this pastor struggled with how to convey the weight of this message in a twenty-first-century context. Finally he took the listener into the scripture passage by using his well-honed coaching techniques: "Imagine the person you love the most in the world. Would you take a beating for them? Now imagine that person taking a beating for you, and there is nothing you can do but stand by and watch."

These coaching questions and images took the listener into a new dimension. After the sermon, several laity noted on our weekend comment cards how moving this sermon was in their spiritual life. This growth occurred through a sermon designed to *coach* the listener rather than *preach at* the listener. As we move into the future, several of us intend to improve our coaching skills and adapt them to the pulpit, because we have identified that our listeners – the postmodern ones, in particular –

prefer being taken into the story. Coaching gives us another tool in our preaching toolbox for connecting with our listeners and bringing God's Word to life.

Postscript

I have been blessed to work on a team of trained coaches of such excellent caliber. These coaches consistently amaze me with their ability to connect and be in relationship with those to whom they are called to minister. Because I have seen first-hand how dynamic and healthy ministries can be when led by a coach, I am signed up for advanced coach training in 2012.

Key Points

- Open yourself to coaching to better yourself and your ministry teams.
- Coaching helps define who your staff members really are – at their core. You will find that your team communicates more openly and understands where other team members are coming from.
- Coaching creates ownership and effectively moves the vision forward.

~~~~~~~~~~~~~~~~~~~~~~~~~

Rev. Jennifer Williams serves as executive pastor of CrossPoint Church, a United Methodist Community. She and her husband, Warren Bevacqua, also a United Methodist minister, graduated from Duke Divinity School and were ordained elder together at the 2002 Central Pennsylvania Annual Conference. Jennifer has a background in social justice and a degree in political science from Temple University in Philadelphia. She is the proud mother of Theadora Grace Bevacqua, born on April 18, 2011. She will attend Coaching4Clergy's Accelerated Coach Training in the fall of 2012.
~~~~~~~~~~~~~~~~~~~~~~~~~

Philippians 1:6

Being confident of this very thing, that He who has begun a good work in you will complete it until the day of Jesus Christ.

SECTION THREE:
Managing Change and Transition

This is a must-read section for every ministry leader. There is a great quote from Myron Madden: "Everyone wants to be fixed; not many want to change." With the ministry platelets already shifting, change is everywhere in the church. Most ministry leaders understand that we must minister differently, yet as Myron says, "Not many want to change."

This section contains real stories of people in ministry who have stepped out in faith and made those necessary changes and shifts. In addition, you will find practical nuts-and-bolts tools to produce the same results in your area of ministry.

My hope is that this section will also encourage additional entrepreneurial approaches to ministry. Interest in spirituality is high in today's world, and yet the average local church is either in recline or decline. Jesus was right when saying, "The harvest is truly great. The laborers are few."

Meaningful Worship: Coaching a Missional Congregation

By Kay L. Kotan

"There is not a single guest who comes through our doors on Sunday who doesn't know how happy we are to welcome him or her and that we want him or her to become a part of the life of our congregation," proudly reported the hospitality team leader with a huge grin on her face. It was apparent that she recognized the fact that it wasn't too long ago that a guest would not have had the same experience she was now reporting. Just one year prior, a guest had reported that while the people in the congregation were friendly, he felt they did not desire a relationship any deeper than a polite, shallow greeting.

Boy, what a difference a year can make! Over this time, it was my privilege and blessing to lead this congregation through implementing some new strategies that were identified through the Missouri Annual Conference of the United Methodist Church's Healthy Church Initiative (HCI) process. This church undergirded the entire process with prayer, and as a result the process has been spirit-filled and met with a sincere desire to be faithful to the work God intended for their church.

Defining coaching can be challenging, but is always an interesting topic of conversation for me, especially with those who have never heard of coaching or experienced it firsthand. Many laity leaders feel that coaching is for the business world and does not fit the mold and/or is not appropriate for use in the church. I always love a challenge, so here is how I define coaching and its usefulness in the church setting:

Coaching allows communication to occur in a new light. First, it identifies the state of a current situation. Second, it identifies the desired outcome of the situation. Finally, it uncovers the action steps that will take the coachee(s) from the current situation to the desired outcome. While sometimes coaching is directive, it is most often a productive process that allows for more possibility, dreams, options, collaboration, accountability, and forward progress – living in the present and moving into the future. A coaching session is time set aside to reflect, learn, strategize, ponder, challenge, stretch, shift, reconsider, and set goals. As coaches, we find that most of our coachees do not allow themselves this much-needed processing time without being in a formal relationship with a coach who is holding them accountable, encouraging them, and calling them to action. Coaching is one of the most powerful development tools available today in both the business world *and* the church!

Here is an outline of how we applied the coaching process to meet the goals of this church:

Visioning

One of the first coaching experiences with this church was leading the laity leaders through the process of casting the vision of their church. They had already accepted "the making of disciples for the transformation of the world" as their mission (purpose). It was now time to determine how they would live that mission in their own unique way over the upcoming three to five years.

This process started with the basic definitions of *mission* and *vision*. But it was during the next steps that God truly started working on the hearts and minds of those gathered in the room. The group was invited to participate in a solo prayer walk in their community (mission field). I asked them to ponder the following questions as they walked and prayed:

- If Jesus were walking alongside you, what would He see, hear, or experience that would break His heart?
- What burdens in your community does your church have the strengths to address?
- What is God placing in your heart as a way to connect to those who are lost?

The participants came back from their prayer walks and were invited to share and record their observations in small group settings. Then each small group displayed a written record of their observations to share with the other groups. It was then that people were able to see and experience their community in a very different and profound manner. You could see hearts softening and hear the shifts in people's thinking as they shared with one another. They brought to life an ownership and a deeper understanding of their commitment to those who are searching. It always gives me chills to lead this process with a church, as I have never walked away without having also been changed in the process myself.

If you are interested in obtaining a complimentary outline of this visioning process, please email me at Kay@KayKotan.com.

Strategic Ministry Planning

Another key strategy in the coaching process was strategic ministry planning – incorporating the five elements of mission, vision, core values, goals, and objectives. We had already established their mission and vision, but still needed to figure out the core values, goals, and objectives.

Core values exist in any organization. Many times they are not named or intentionally followed, but if we carefully examine the criteria used in our decision-making process, we can uncover these core values. Often core values are revealed that leaders are not necessarily thrilled to name or own. This is when we begin to explore the core values that the leaders aspire to grow into as a church. This questioning process almost always creates lively conversation among the leaders. Often this type of self-examination had been ignored.

Leaders are usually grateful to get to the step of naming their church goals – finally they can sink their teeth into something solid! This is when I lead the board/council into naming those three to five goals that will help them live their vision and accomplish the mission while living within the boundaries of their core values. I always suggest that the first goal address how many people they will reach out to in the mission field in the upcoming year – how many lost sheep will they bring into the life of their congregation? This helps the group navigate their definition of *reaching* –

is it baptism, attending an event, or somewhere in between? It also helps them see reaching the mission field as a responsibility of their church. This is usually a pivotal moment for some real shifts in people's thoughts and feelings. You can see the Spirit at work as people wrestle with the questions as a group and also in their own individual hearts and minds.

It can be difficult for church leaders to set goals that are overarching for the entire church. They tend to want to talk about individual ministries, events, programs, or positions. The time for those conversations is later. There will be plenty of time, since setting goals is a pathway that the church will journey along in the next year to bring them closer to the picture of the preferred future that was identified in their vision statement.

I ask people to use the S.M.A.R.T. acronym to make sure their goals are complete, informative, and measureable. The acronym stands for specific, measurable, achievable, relevant, and time-based. This is a great measuring tool for ensuring the goals are complete.

The final piece of the strategic ministry process is objectives. Objectives can be described as the action steps needed to accomplish the goals. This is when the detail-oriented people really kick into gear. It is during this step that ministry teams take ownership of accomplishing or partially accomplishing a goal. By doing this as the last step, the team already has clarity about how their annual activities will tie into the church's overall goals. Objectives are an intricate piece of the puzzle for accomplishing the church's mission through its vision and goals, with all working together for a common purpose. The objectives step is a reflection of the church's ministry, when all the outwardly-focused action takes place through the individual hands of the congregation.

The first time a church takes the journey of engaging in strategic ministry planning, it is usually quite time-consuming. I have found that creating a color-coded series of posters depicting all the pieces of the process is quite helpful. This visual aid shows the participants how each piece fits together to make up the "big picture" of the church's purpose and activities for the year.

When new ideas emerge during the year, the church now has a strategic method for determining whether the idea should be embraced and put into action or shelved for another day. The key question leaders begin to use is, "How does this idea/action/activity/program move us towards accomplishing our goals for this year?" It's no longer a matter of saying yes to everyone and everything out of fear of hurting someone's feelings. Instead, decisions are based on the organization's purpose.

If you are interested in a resource to help guide you through strategic ministry planning, please visit www.KayKotan.com.

Prayer Team

One of the first steps in preparing for the United Methodist Church's Healthy Church Initiative (HCI) process is to put together a prayer team. Prayer teams, of course, are not new to churches. However, they are traditionally assembled to pray for those in the congregation going through difficult times. The HCI Prayer Team is asked to pray for the mission field, community leaders (such as firemen, policemen, city leaders, teachers, principals, etc.), and those who are lost. This team is challenged to be outwardly focused in their prayers.

This particular Prayer Team took the challenge to heart with gusto and enthusiasm. First they sought a special place in their church to pray. They convinced a Sunday school class to relocate so that the chapel could be converted to a prayer room. They then redecorated the chapel with prayer stations reflecting the current needs of the community. To this day, they continue to update these prayer stations to reflect the community's current needs and concerns. This prayer chapel has taken this congregation to a higher level of prayer and outward focus.

From the very beginning of my consultation weekend with this church, it felt different. The atmosphere was warmer, more inviting, and more comfortable. We were taken on a building tour that included the new prayer chapel. (I still get goose bumps just telling the story!) When I walked into the chapel, I saw four prayer stations. One station displayed all the community leaders' individual names, along with a suggested prayer. You could sit or kneel, and there was soft lighting and calming music playing in the background. The next station named each of the police officers and fire workers in the community. The next station had articles and information about a horrific tornado that had hit in the region, along with a suggested prayer. The last station had each of our consultants' names on tent cards, asking for prayers of wisdom, guidance, and discernment for the weekend. There was also an open Bible, a candle, and a suggested prayer.

That weekend was met with such openness, sense of purpose, knowing, and believing. The report was much easier to write than others had been. The atmosphere and people were spirit-filled. Worship was meaningful and touching. Yes, God was in the building and in the hearts of the congregation that weekend. No doubt!

Coaching this pastor and church through this process allowed me to see God at work in such a beautiful and unique way. The coaching moved people individually into new and deeper relations with God. It moved groups into a new way of believing in and immersing themselves in ministry. It allowed people in the congregation to identify their unique, God-given, spiritual gifts, and how those gifts can be used to build God's Kingdom. It brought the church together for a common mission and vision with a renewed spirit and bountiful energy. They are now a church of purpose, and no longer merely a building on the edge of town.

~~~~~~~~~~~~~~~~~~~~~~~~~~

Kay L. Kotan is a certified coach, a graduate of Coach U and Advanced Coach U, and a member of the International Coach Federation (ICF) and the Heartland Coaching Association. She is also the author of *Renovate or Die*, *Full Schedules Barren Souls*, *Insights on Productivity*, and *Strategic Ministry Planning*. She serves on the Executive Team for the Healthy Church Initiative and as faculty for Coaching4Clergy. For more information about speaking, coaching, and consulting, please visit www.KayKotan.com.
~~~~~~~~~~~~~~~~~~~~~~~~~~

True to Their Calling: Coaching for a Sure Start

By Michael Godfrey

How Stephen Stayed True to His Calling

Stephen was bright, perceptive, and people-oriented. He had a degree in business from one of the leading business schools in the nation and was completing his seminary studies. At the same time, he worked as an intern at a mega-church. Stephen was planning to enter full-time ministry – maybe.

His business training, acumen, and sheer talent led him to question leadership actions he experienced at the church. "They do things that don't make sense," he would say. Also at issue was the stress of the eighty-hour work weeks his role required and how this influenced his perception of congregational ministry for his future.

After two years of urging from others who witnessed his stress and struggle that he adjust to ministry demands, Stephen called and engaged in a coaching relationship with me. He related:

> "Pride kept me from meeting with you for a long time. [If I met with you] I had to admit that I didn't have it all together and that I needed someone to help me. Clergy try too hard to look like they always have it all together, never struggle, and can handle everything that comes their way. But clergy are regular people, just like everyone else."

We quickly developed a trusting, open relationship. Early on, there seemed to be an undercurrent of questions on Stephen's part about whether congregational ministry was really for him. Flowing along with these questions was concern about the time he had spent getting a seminary education being a waste if he took a different career path. He enjoyed web design and was currently being paid to work on a few sites.

In one session I asked Stephen, "What motivated you to pursue congregational ministry as a career path?" There was silence and Stephen shifted in his chair.

"Well, I guess I just really had a great high school youth group at my church and a great youth minister. I thought it would be really neat to do something like that. It's not as neat as I thought."

We talked for a good while about how, with his fiery interests, talents, and gifts, he could serve God with all of his heart in a career other than congregational ministry. He wondered how he could be "true to his calling" and do this.

I offered Stephen what coaches call a direct message, stating my own opinion about calling. He did not need to agree at all; I simply placed this on the table as an alternative way of thinking about the situation.

I believe that all Christians have only one calling and many occupations. The Christian calling is to be Christ in the world to the glory of God. This can be done in many ways, and through many occupations. In fact, in some situations, for some people, the Kingdom of God may be served better through an occupation other than congregational ministry or a religious occupation.

As I shared this, Stephen's face and energy changed. This direct message seemed to create some new awareness and open a freedom he had lost at some point in the past.

"Stephen, if you could do anything you wanted to do with your career at this point, without any restrictions, what would you do?"

"I'd open a web design company and do that full time."

He started his company a very short time later and continues to do well with it. He lives out his vocation through his business, making wonderful contributions to the Kingdom of God. Here's what he says, in retrospect, about coaching:

> "... [coaching] provided me with a safe outlet to decompress and address work-related conflicts, relationship stresses, and other factors that negatively affected my day-to-day and provided valuable resources and practices to help me improve in areas such as time-management, stress relief, and self-awareness that have made a positive impact on my ability to be successful in the areas of life that are most important to me, including my business. "

"Go for Coaching or Fail Your Course."

Ian was in his early twenties and struggling with school and life in general. He was approaching graduation from a southeastern university. Pursuing a career in congregational ministry, he had already had one unsuccessful work experience in a church. He was currently serving as pastor of a very small church while finishing school.

He was referred to me by his university professor who knew about my work coaching clergy. His professor paid for the coaching and told Ian that unless he coached with me for six weeks, he would fail the class.

Since the coaching was mandatory for Ian, he was less than forthcoming in the beginning. Eventually I learned that he was a pastor's son. I asked him about how he came to the ministerial career path. He openly shared that he was in a drug-induced high when he experienced "the call." With no judgment, I asked questions in an attempt to generate reflection on the call and how authentic he believed it to be. This conversation went on for a couple of sessions.

From an intuitive prompt, and without any agenda, I asked Ian, "Is there a chance that before we end our time together you will say, 'God has not called me to career ministry after all'?"

With his face toward the table, he looked out of the tops of his eyes and said, "Can you do that? Can a person do that?"

I told him, "Yes, you can."

"Then, yes. There is a chance," he said.

After several weeks of reflection, the subject was raised again and Ian expressed confidence that he would continue to pursue a career in congregational ministry.

I asked Ian to evaluate our time together. He said, "At first, I felt judged." As we talked this through, he related that he had learned to trust me and no longer felt judged. He also related, "You ask hard questions." The questions were hard because they required him to think, and to think about his thinking.

Ian passed the course and graduated, and at last word is happily married, expecting a first child, doing remodeling work, and happy as can be.

Encounters such as these are common for me since a part of my practice is work with seminarians and those just beginning a religious career in early adulthood. How do I best serve these bright and committed young individuals?

First and foremost, I believe I best serve this group through profound respect. I respect them as growing adults who are capable, whole, and full of potential. I respect their thoughts and opinions as evidence of individuality and autonomy. I project this through my manner with them and through verbal acknowledgement. This respect contributes strongly to the coaching relationship elements of intimacy and trust. My respect for my coachees also fuels my confidence in their being in the driver's seat, while I am happy to ride along with them.

I also serve them by helping them think critically. Idealism is a developmental issue for them, which is sometimes expressed in limited black and white terms, and sometimes expressed dogmatically. Most often this thinking is comprised of assumptions that have not been examined critically. Some were inherited as conventional thinking and some were created as an attempt to make sense of things. The lack of critical examination is partially due to incomplete neurological development and partially due to lack of skill. If these assumptions are left undisturbed, the individual will likely carry them further into adulthood, creating limitations on their development in the various stages of their adult life.

I can help them think critically about their assumptions and beliefs, and about their thinking itself. I do this by asking powerful questions, providing silence as time to think, and listening deeply and respectfully.

I acknowledge that the urge to be parental and tell the coachee the "best" way to think or the "best" thing to do can be one of the greatest temptations when coaching this age group, especially given the age differential. Since these are spiritual issues, there is also the temptation to be pastoral and "tell" from the position of pastoral authority. But to influence coachees in these ways would be a betrayal of the coaching role. It is essential that the coach be fully present with them without thinking ahead, and be non-judgmental and without an agenda. You can be a parent or pastor – and neither is wrong – or you can be a coach. But you cannot be both.

I find that today's young adults are interested in the benefits that can be gained from the experience of older adults, including coaches and mentors. Young people want to make good decisions, but realize that they're lacking the information and confidence that can only come from experience. They are not usually open to advice unless advice is invited.

Generally a coach takes care to avoid offering advice to a coachee. Why waste the breath, especially since it is rumored that less than 1 percent of advice is taken? We just can't know what is best in each coachee's unique situation. Instead the coach can state, "This is how I have seen it work for others," or "This is how it worked for me," and let the coachee learn vicariously as desired. I can help my coachees by offering such insights from my experience. Sometimes, if it's appropriate and requested, I can also offer advice.

It is a developmental essential that coachees find their own answers. I use questions to assist them, not only in finding their answers but also in calling forth critical thinking skills for problem solving and living responsibly. "How did you come to that thinking?" is a question I use frequently. With this question, I am calling on them to think about their thinking. As a coach, I listen deeply and paraphrase back what I hear. This allows me to support the coachee in working through their thinking as they progress through this point in their faith development and look for a career in which they can best serve the Kingdom of God. They are on a journey, deciding on their direction as they reach crucial turning points. I stand alongside and support with a helpful process of coaching. Both of the coachees I described above discovered their own answers and their own way, and are happy about it. And they believe God is, too.

Once these individuals find their answers, I can best help them by supporting them to design actions and move toward their goals. So it has been with Stephen as he has excelled as a businessman.

Individuals who have a deep love for God and a commitment to Him may believe that the highest expression of this love and commitment is to enter a full-time religious career, and that's what they want to give. This is a false assumption that limits what individuals believe about how they can best serve God. Some who choose a religious career discover through experience that such a career path is just not a fit for them, but they continue in it to their misery and to the detriment of their congregations. It is entirely possible that these individuals may best live out their calling in a career other than religion or church. If they choose another occupation, they are no less in the eyes of God. Remember that God has used shepherds, fig-pickers, tent-makers, and fishermen, all to his Glory and the expansion of His eternal Kingdom.

Here are some additional coaching tools for reaching out to young adults who are trying to be faithful to God and experience a satisfying career:

- Build relationships with this generation.
- Be genuinely interested.
- Show them your highest respect.
- Avoid judgment or agenda.
- Listen much.
- Give advice only when asked for and when appropriate.
- Be a sounding board as they design action plans.
- Stay available to them.

~~~~~~~~~~~~~~~~~~~~~~~~~~
~~~~~~~~~~~~~~~~~~~~~~~~~~

J. Michael Godfrey, D.Min., Ph.D., ACC
True Course Life & Leadership Development
Coach/Speaker/Mentor/Consultant

Consistently recognized as a gifted leader and as an authority in the field of adult learning and development, Dr. Michael Godfrey expertly uses mentoring and coaching to assist nationally renowned organizations and their leaders to "be more, see more, and achieve more." Dr. Godfrey's approach received the Malcolm S. Knowles Award from the American Association of Adult and Continuing Education. He is founder and president of True Course, a senior consultant for the Birkman method, and serves as a lecturer at the George W. Truett Theological Seminary. www.discoveryourtruecourse.com

From Burnout to Breakthrough: Coaching for a Faithful Finish

By Michael Godfrey

It was an overcast, dreary, crawl-back-in-bed kind of day in December. I sensed that the situation was not much different inside of Phil as he passed my table while exiting a local restaurant.

As he hurried out the door we exchanged greetings, and he said, "Hey, I need to call you after Christmas. I may want to use your services."

"You bet, Phil! I'll look forward to it." Phil knew that I was a coach who often worked with clergy. He left me wondering what was up.

At the time, Phil was a busy fifty-three-year-old pastor of an 800-member congregation. He was capable and well-trained. He was the only full-time staff person at his church, and supervised several part-time staff members. During his seventeen-year tenure, the church had grown in every way.

He and I did make contact and we agreed I would coach him in person in his office at the church. He paid for the services out of his own pocket, which to me was evidence of his great interest in finding some resolution and peace in his situation. He insisted on buying my lunch on several occasions after our sessions.

During our first visit, it was evident that Phil was confused and had many questions about his future. He sensed pressure from the church deacons to provide more visionary leadership and get the church moving.

This pressure came at a time when his mental and emotional resources were exhausted. Phil's self-doubt and burn-out was fueled by the demands of pastoral leadership and the rest of his life coming toward him at full force. He wife worked at a high-stress job. His father had been experiencing a long-term decline in health. On his weekly days off, Phil drove several hours each way to provide care for his father and mother. Then his father died. He moved his mother to live with his family in a house that was too small to accommodate them all, so he was called on to sell his house, doing all the work himself to fix it up for the sale. After buying a new house, he was responsible for two house payments for quite some time before the old house sold.

In the meantime, there were issues at work. A staff member came under fire and resigned under pressure. Phil recognized that his perfectionism and difficulty with fully delegating responsibility along with authority were contributing to his burned-out state. In addition, church members were fussy about things like the community kids using the church property for skateboarding, something Phil saw as an opportunity to reach the kids.

He told me he just couldn't come up with any vision, and he wondered if he could continue to pastor the church. He was burned out.

"So, Phil," I inquired, "What are your options?"

He said, "You know, I suppose I could stay here and continue to fight the fight and try to cast vision. I could go to another church, but I am not sure I have another one in me, and at my age, the market is limited. I don't have training or experience to do anything else."

Over several sessions, Phil reflected on his experience as I listened deeply and asked questions to achieve clarity and encourage his thinking. He continued to assert that he could not get in touch with any vision for the church. "I just don't have it in me."

I asked his permission to state what I was noticing and he agreed I could. I said, "Phil, you seem to be trying to run on fumes and are too busy to think. The vision is in there, it just needs some space to surface."

Then, at the beginning of a session, without realizing what he had done, Phil said, "I want this church to be known as a church that shares the love and grace of Christ with this community."

"Say that again, Phil," I requested.

"I want this church to be known as a church that shares the love and grace of Christ with this community."

"Do you realize what you just did?"

"Well, no, uh, uh."

"You just stated your vision for the church. Say that again."

"I want this church to be known as a church that shares the love and grace of Christ with this community."

Phil was a little bit giddy at that point. He'd had a major breakthrough and almost took it for granted.

In time, Phil added a new staff member, took some time off, and gained enough mental and emotional clarity to make quality decisions for him and for the church. In addition, he is actively sharing leadership with his team at the church, which is currently more supportive of his leadership. The church even provided him with a six-week sabbatical leave at their initiative.

My dream is that pastors like Phil will build a habit of reaching out for a regular sharpening influence in their lives and careers in an effort to promote wellness in the whole of their beings – social, emotional, physical, and spiritual. What I most commonly see, however, is that the pain quotient must be very high in order for a pastor to reach out. Quite often, by that point, their options for growth and health have been reduced significantly. I prefer wellness over the hospital every time.

As I reflect on my experience with Phil, I note that a number of core elements of the coaching process were powerfully at play in supporting him in addressing his needs and moving to action. The International Coach Federation sets forth eleven competencies, but I was careful not to force the competencies as an agenda for Phil's coaching.

Phil was experiencing one of the most powerful challenges faced by clergy – isolation. Another pastor of a large congregation told me, in a very objective and detached fashion, that he had no real friends and that he had reached out to three people outside of his situation and congregation in whom to confide.

Clergy often hold themselves to an unrealistic standard in the whole of their lives. Some clergy are reluctant to reach out for help, fearful that such an act would indicate that they are deficient in some area, making them vulnerable to criticism from the congregation.

From their research, Hill, Darling, and Raimondi note:

> "[Clergy] are put on this pedestal of invincibility, which has the secondary gain of grandiosity; however, it also leaves them feeling lonely and isolated. Clergy tended to feel isolated from the rest of the community and reported feeling a sense of loneliness and vulnerability within their communities."*

It truly is lonely at the top, whether in congregations or businesses. For leaders in congregations, however, the opportunity to openly share with others around them may be even more limited than in some businesses. One misunderstanding or disagreement with what a pastor says can lead to a downward spiral in credibility and, in the worst case, loss of income, medical benefits, and housing. Consequently, members of the clergy are often guarded about what they say, and the people available for them to confide in are limited.

When clergy have no one in whom to confide about the challenges and frustrations of congregational leadership, their mental processes can run toward the reactive and anxious. Things get bigger than they are in reality, assumptions are perceived as truth, worry escalates, and insecurity deepens.

Intimacy, trust, presence, and deep listening are the core coaching competencies that Phil needed from me in the face of his isolation. He needed a third party, unattached to his situation, with whom he could be completely open with his frustrations, pain, and doubt. He needed assurance that confidentiality would rule the day. He also needed someone who could be with him for the sake of being with him versus someone meeting with him to promote an agenda, press judgment, tell him something, solve his problem, fix him, or serve as a consultant.

Phil was more than capable of finding his own way; he had been doing so for a long time. At this time, however, he did need some support and encouragement to rise out of the maelstrom of challenges he faced. I see this as the role of *paraklete* – one called alongside to help. Certainly Holy paraklete was living and working in both of us, but sometimes we need the paraklete "with skin on." I was privileged to be this for Phil.

Phil needed time to think. To a large extent, congregations are not thinking environments. They are emotional, reactive, and busy, and busy-ness is viewed as equal to productivity and health. Congregations feel that if "nothing is happening," somebody is not doing their job. Clergy are usually very capable thinkers in some areas. But they have a 24/7 busy-ness that contributes to a thinking deficit. They don't have time to think. When they do think, their ideas are introduced into an emotional and reactive congregation that discourages thinking. And so it goes.

"Everything we do depends on the thinking we do first and our thinking depends on the quality of our attention for each other," says Nancy Kline in her book *Time to Think*.** If this is true, and clergy do not have time to think, what kind of decisions must they be making?

As a coach, I created a safe space – a parenthesis in Phil's busy schedule – in which he could take time to think. In addition, I listened much and deeply. I sensed that he had few opportunities to experience this. I also employed questions that would prompt further thought and challenge Phil to think about his thinking, which may have become clouded by his situation. As a result, his statement of vision surfaced as almost a surprise to him.

Age and experience do not equal awareness. The stress of congregational leadership can lead to chronic, low-level anxiety and periodic high anxiety during which the bigger picture is hard to comprehend. It can be very easy to lose sight of the forest for the trees in congregational leadership. Coaching can help clergy engage more rational function, yielding increased awareness of the various components of self and situation and helping them to ask, "How else can I look at this?"

Phil needed affirmation. He was looking back and wondering if he had made a real difference. He was looking forward and wondering if he could finish well.

When clergy reach their fifties, transition and retirement is in view, and two questions commonly loom in their heads regarding their leadership of congregations. One is, "Can I hold out to finish this one?" The other is, "If I don't finish here, do I have another one of these in me?" These questions are often born out of the fact that most clergy are trained for the clergy, and that's it. If they leave congregational leadership at fifty-five and need to seek employment outside of church or denominational service, it requires retraining. Some, like Phil, gain a renewed vision. Others, to their detriment and that of their congregations, just fasten their seatbelts, flip the autopilot switch, and hope to survive on their past merits until retirement.

I acknowledged Phil for his faithful and effective work, which had become a faded memory in the midst of his current turmoil. I also acknowledged my belief that he still had much to offer his congregation. Accessing the services of a good coach can help clergy find renewed vision and its associated actions. They can also discover next steps in their calling if continuing at the current congregation is not an option. This creates the path to a faithful finish in the "calling to which they have been called."

I also saw that Phil could benefit from some extreme self-care. My sense is that most clergy hold the false assumption that caring deeply for yourself is selfish and a sin. Further, some live under the limiting belief that if they stay busy, they will produce more. I supported Phil as he designed actions toward self-care and building reserves for his physical, spiritual, social, emotional, and intellectual being. We explored what he had done to this point and the results of it. Then we explored what he might do in the future and the results that might bring. Phil determined to take actions that would build those reserves.

I highly respect Phil for reaching out. It would have been easy for someone in his situation to get on the glide path toward retirement, only doing what was necessary to keep his job. But this was not Phil's way. He was clearly a learner and a seeker of answers. He said, "[Coaching] is meeting real needs and filling the gaps, not only for young ministers needing to get their feet on the ground early, but also for seasoned pastors like myself who may need a listening ear or a new set of eyes to look at persistent challenges."

Phil reached inside himself to find courage to reach out for support and encouragement in the dark times. I am privileged to serve him as he continues to lead his congregation to greater health and growth, and looks forward to hearing a "Well done!" to a faithful finish in Kingdom leadership.

You can serve seasoned pastors like Phil with a coach approach by:

- Being available
- Inquiring about how they are *really* doing and silently waiting for their response
- Creating a safe, non-judgmental place for them to talk about their deepest concerns and common frustrations
- Listening with genuine interest
- Supporting them in efforts to take extreme care of themselves
- Acknowledging, affirming, and encouraging more than you think is needed

If you are a member of their congregation:

- Help and encourage them to find a coach, therapist, and/or other confidant with whom to meet regularly, in person or by phone.
- Encourage the church to provide financial resources to support those options.

~~~~~~~~~~~~~~~~~~~~~~~~~

*Hill, E.W., Darling, C.A., & Raimondi, N.M. (2003). "Understanding Boundary-Related Stress in Clergy Families." *Marriage & Family Review*, 35(1/2), 147-166.

**Kline, N. (2001). *Time to Think*. London: Cassell Illustrated. P. 17

Consistently recognized as a gifted leader and as an authority in the field of adult learning and development, Dr. Michael Godfrey expertly uses mentoring and coaching to assist nationally renowned organizations and their leaders to "be more, see more, and achieve more." Dr. Godfrey's approach received the Malcolm S. Knowles Award from the American Association of Adult and Continuing Education. He is founder and president of True Course, a senior consultant for the Birkman method, and serves as a lecturer at the George W. Truett Theological Seminary. www.discoveryourtruecourse.com
~~~~~~~~~~~~~~~~~~~~~~~~~

Growing Beyond the Lid: Coaching the Multi-Site Church

By C. Darrell Roland

Community First Church had been growing at an average rate of 13.2 percent over the past eight years, and building another facility was not an option. The leadership team had been struggling with what to do about this dilemma. In *The 21 Irrefutable Laws of Leadership*, leadership consultant and former pastor John Maxwell describes "the law of the lid" as the fact that every leader or leadership team has a ceiling, and once they've reached it, the organization cannot grow beyond that point. While the Community First Church team desired to hang on to their momentum of growth, they realized they were closing in on their own "lid," and that lid was space.

Executive Pastor Mark saw this as an opportunity to grow into their community more by creating multi-site campuses throughout the city. Many of his colleagues around the country were doing this successfully and he really felt this was the way for the church to capitalize on their momentum with minimal upfront expense. Community First's lead pastor, Pastor Jeff, also felt that the multi-site campus model was where God was leading them.

Since Community First desired to be led by God, they launched an additional site with a campus pastor who delivered the message instead of employing the more traditional model in which the lead pastor is on video for the message.

Initially they opened one additional campus, and it experienced slow but steady growth with a solid core group. Then an opportunity arose to purchase a neighboring community-based church that was in trouble. Over a long and arduous process of due diligence and financial acquisition, Community First purchased the facility. The initial plan was for the lead pastor to speak at the home campus at 8:00am and 9:00am, and then go to the new campus to speak at 10:45am, and then go back to the main campus for a noon service. Yes, four services at two locations each Sunday morning!

While leadership knew this was not the best answer for the long term, they felt it was an opportunity they could not pass up and that pleased those who preferred a small congregation but wanted to pioneer something new. Over time, the new site was assigned a speaking campus pastor as well; again, not as traditional multi-site ministries do, but capitalizing on an opportunity.

A few years later, Community First found itself running out of space at their original campus again. The leadership discussed their options, and once again felt their vision was to launch more sites. This time, they had more time to plan and a few years of experience to help guide their decision process. They began looking at potential sites for a multi-site campus with a video message and live worship. Based on all they had learned from the initial launches and new resources for this future purpose, they felt this was the best option.

Why Multi-Site Coaching?

Church growth is an ongoing challenge in today's culture. We live in a society that is becoming more active on social media, while becoming less social. We have increasing financial challenges. Many Americans are either out of work or have not seen financial growth in several years due to the state of our economy. We preach that we live in a different kingdom than the world, and that is true; we live in a kingdom in which we trust that God is our protector and provider. However, the average person cannot connect that idea to his or her troubled life. So how can the church operate in the societal kingdom and not forsake the expansion of the Kingdom of God?

Churches are stuck in the old paradigm of thinking that we have to either stay where we are, plant a church, or build a building. Yet the cost of building another facility is often out of reach. The endurance and time needed for planting a church exceeds our energy levels, while studies show that at least 80 percent of church plants fail. In addition, a good church plant can take several years to become self-sufficient.

Feeling discouraged by those realities has opened the minds of some congregations to consider multi-site churches as another option – an option that they have probably heard of, but may be skeptical about. "They're just a fad," some say. Well, maybe so, but why not partake in the move of God while He is working there? Hundreds of churches have moved into a multi-site structure due to the economic challenges facing our churches today.

With church leadership struggling to envision how they can implement the multi-site structure within their church DNA, there is a great opportunity for coaching support. The coach's role is not to implement the multi-site, but to coach the multi-site leadership team in making the best decision for their church. Just as the purpose of coaching is to come alongside a person to help them develop their best path, so it is with coaching the multi-site church option.

In the balance of this chapter we will discuss two areas of multi-site church coaching: the potential multi-site church, and the existing multi-site church. While your approach may be similar, there will be some distinct differences as you express your unique gifts. Above all, you can strive to help every minister and ministry to walk this journey and avoid the pitfalls before them.

Potential Multi-Site Churches

These churches have not implemented a plan for launching a multi-site church, but have begun to discuss the idea. When a church is not coached through this process, there is the potential for it to either become divided – two churches under the same roof – or to meander slowly along towards the goal of being one church with one vision. Either path will be costly to their ministry. When this distinction goes unaddressed, the multi-site campus can become disconnected and even disjointed from its origins. That's why coaching at this stage can be very effective in accomplishing the desired results.

Regardless of how hard we try, square pegs do not fit in round holes without reshaping or painful force. You may find that multi-site does not fit in the existing culture of a church, and it will be very beneficial to identify that today rather than after three years of strife in multi-site ministry.

Most churches step out into whatever has been done before, whatever others are doing, or whatever God opens up for them. Let me be clear; I am not saying that either of the above is wrong or ineffective. I am saying that because every church, every congregation, and every leader has a different story, there is no cookie-cutter plan for success. Coaching can help a church and church leadership find their path to multi-site. Not all paths are the same and not all paths are for every church. Coaching the potential multi-site church helps the congregation intentionally infuse their future with their DNA. If a growing church is healthy, with healthy leadership, it is in their best interest to ensure the DNA carries over into their future multi-site campuses. This will raise the platform of success for the sites.

Coaching the Leader

Research statistics show us that being a lead pastor or leader is clearly one of the loneliest positions. There are few places outside of their "fishbowl" where they can share their thoughts, feelings, and ideas. Proverbs 18:1 tells us that "a man who isolated himself, seeks his own desire," yet I wonder how many isolated leaders have absolutely zero desire to seek their own desire; it's just that they lack a safe place to brainstorm. Create a safe place where the lead pastor or the multi-site leader can share, dream, and emerge from the fishbowl. In many instances, this clears the mind for creativity and vision to flow.

Coaching the Leadership

Gather the leadership together for coaching sessions to define the future of furthering the vision of the church. Create an open environment for discussion for leadership. Often in churches we use the term *koinonia* loosely; however, back in the days of Socrates, they had three firm rules to govern these fellowship meetings: 1) No arguing 2) No interrupting

3) Listen carefully. Socrates and his friends gathered together for years sharing ideas and perspectives without any intent of changing each other's minds or perspectives. Help the church leadership create an atmosphere of koinonia in their group coaching sessions. This will without a doubt foster an environment in which God can help the leaders intentionally define their path of growth.

Questions for Potential Multi-Site Churches

1. What pieces of DNA have fostered your current health and growth?
2. What pieces of DNA have fostered your current frustration and hindrance?
3. How do you want to use this growth internally and externally?
4. Who do you have to become as a leader/leadership/church in order for this to come to fruition?
5. Who/what are some resources you can tap in to for help?
6. What do you absolutely know today about your next steps?
7. What do you need to know in order to take your next steps?
8. What is the absolute must-do date for the next step?
9. If you had to step out today, what would that step be?
10. What has kept you from moving forward thus far?

Existing Multi-Site Churches

While your coaching methods and even much of your approach will remain the same, there are a few underlying elements that need to be included when coaching existing multi-site churches. They are already in the midst of managing a multi-site ministry, and as in the example of Community First Church above, it may not be what they had intended. While the temptation may be to determine why they are where they are, a coach's only goal is to help them determine where they want to go. This ensures that no time is spent looking backward with blame. You want a blame-free environment that will be forward focused.

Coaching the Leader

As stated earlier, there are few places where lead pastors and leaders can share their thoughts, feelings, and ideas outside of their fishbowl. Your job here, again, is to create a safe place for the lead pastor or the multi-site leader to share, dream, and emerge from the fishbowl. You want leaders to feel free to say whatever they desire so they can get objective feedback and not allow their feelings to become their guides. If the sites are successful, isolation can create pride. If the sites are less than successful, they can develop a feeling of failure. Neither of these are helpful in nourishing the future of existing sites or future ones. Focus on the leader as a person, coach the best in them, and help them find the best in themselves.

Coaching the Leadership

As with potential multi-site churches, you want to coach the leadership group around the future of furthering the vision of the church. However, it is crucial to understand that personal values have been incorporated into multi-site campus definitions, so people may be sensitive about discussing potential changes. Before a group coaching session, you may find it helpful to set up some ground rules up front. Evaluate the group and determine what rules they want to implement. The practice of koinonia may be all you need.

Questions for Existing Multi-Site Churches

1. What brought you to become a multi-site ministry?
2. What steps were taken as you implemented multi-site ministry in your church?
3. What pleases you about your current multi-site ministry?

4. What are your tolerations and frustrations about your current multi-site campuses?
5. What did you envision as you launched multi-site in your church?
6. How is your current reality aligning with your desired outcome?
7. What changes would you make if you could flip a switch and they would be done?
8. Who do you have to become as a leader/leadership/church for this to come to fruition?
9. Who/what are some resources you can tap in to for help?
10. What has kept you from moving forward thus far? How will you navigate that?

Conclusion

As in all coaching, there are a multitude of paths to coach on the subject of multi-site ministry; these are only a few. If you are considering a multi-site ministry, I encourage you to find a coach to help you navigate the decisions before you. If you are the coach of such a church, I encourage you to stay completely open to what God is saying to the congregation about their path. Coaching can facilitate and expedite the process of fulfilling all that God has laid before these churches.

~~~~~~~~~~~~~~~~~~~~~~~~
~~~~~~~~~~~~~~~~~~~~~~~~

C. Darrell Roland, PCC, CCA, spent twenty years in industrial and corporate environments prior to moving into ministry where he has served the past eleven years as an executive pastor for a growing multi-site church. He became a certified church administrator through the National Association of Church Business Administration (NACBA) and Candler Theological Institute. He completed his coaching studies at Coach U and Coaching4Clergy, and he is accredited as a professional certified coach with the International Coach Federation. He serves as faculty at Coaching4Clergy, where he is a trainer, class facilitator, coach, and mentor coach to pastors and ministry leaders.

Darrell is co-founder of Red Pin Ministries where he and his team serve churches in a variety of areas including accounting services, consulting, strategy, vision, and organizational structure.

darrell.roland@Coaching4Clergy.com

Coaching to the Promised Land: Coaching the Transition to a New Pastor

By Ed Hale

For the first time in years, members were excited about attending a special church meeting with the Transition Team. No one was expecting it to be a typical business meeting with boring reports and long speeches. Instead, there was so much expectation in the air you would think there was going to be a public execution. And I was afraid it was going to be mine.

After their last pastor resigned, I accepted the offer to be a *consultant*, and assist this church in working through a special program called the Intentional Interim Ministry. It was a twelve- to eighteen-month process of getting the church ready for their next pastor and training the search committee to find the right pastor for their next period of history. It required a Transition Team comprised of church members who would lead the church through this "wilderness experience" and enter the "Promised Land" with a new pastor.

I was excited about starting my fifth interim pastorate and began training this church-elected Transition Team to tackle the job. Armed with my training notebook and what I thought was plenty of experience, we began to migrate this large congregation to the land flowing with milk and honey. It started out great. If I could just trust the process and not lead the church into any major life-threatening decisions, we would arrive safely across the Jordan in a few months.

In one of the first meetings with the Transition Team chairperson, I asked if I could *coach* him and the team through this process. He gladly accepted, though he only had a vague understanding of coaching. As we defined the coaching agreement, we concluded that I was not going to tell the Transition Team what to do or make decisions for them, but that I would maintain the process.

Through the training, the team was learning how to discuss their available options and decide as a group how to carry out each team-chosen activity. When the team failed to reach a consensus, they would turn to me and asked what I thought. Within a few sessions, team members would remind each other with the statement, "Don't ask him, he won't tell you!" As graciously as I knew how, I explained that it did not matter what I thought, because I was not going to be around after the church called another pastor – they would have to live with their own decisions – and that what I would do might be very different from what they would do in a similar situation. As lay people, never before had they faced such freedom and responsibility.

One of the team activities was to address the unresolved issues that were lingering in the church. They invited all members to bring their own lists of issues to a special meeting. The Transition Team explained that there would be no discussion at this meeting, but that the process would determine which issues the church would address over the next few months in special meetings. Small groups were assembled at tables where people could share their individual concerns, and then the team compiled everyone's thoughts into one large master list.

At their next meeting, the Transition Team began to panic. What would they do with such a long list of inflammatory issues? Certainly even trying to discuss them all would cause a riot in the church, much less addressing them. If past business meetings were any indication, the team was certain that bringing these issues to a church-wide meeting would result in chaos. After an hour of allowing the team to debate the pros and cons of going forward, I asked a simple question: "What would happen if you trusted the church members to freely discuss the issues openly with each other?" At first, answers ranged from "chaos" to "I don't know!" Then, in a moment of awareness, they suddenly decided to trust the church to *be the church*. Carefully weighing the cost, they decided to proceed with the risk.

The next question was critical. I asked, "Who is the best person to lead these open discussions with the church?" As people pointed fingers and discussed the pros and cons of different choices, the group's fear was mounting. Then someone surprised me and asked, "Would you *coach* the church through these discussions – like you coach us?" I immediately went into internal shock, while practicing a neutral look on my face. I was comfortable coaching one on one and in a small group, but I was not sure about coaching the entire congregation on such hot topics! Trying to be brave and not show my personal fear and trembling, I smiled and said, "Sure." However, deep down there was a reluctance in my soul.

Escaping to my office, I began to ask myself, "Where in church life is there an opportunity for a congregation to share thoughts and feelings in a non-threatening environment?" I could not come up with one. In this church, business meetings were the only possibility, and had historically proved disastrous. Now I was stepping into the arena to face the "lions and tigers and bears – oh my!"

Prior to the first Sunday night's "Main Event" (later to be renamed "Dialogue with the Pastor"), I reviewed my notes on group coaching and knelt in prayer to ask for divine intervention. I instructed the Transition Team that if I coached the congregation, they would need to sit near the front at every discussion – listening intently, taking notes, and participating in the discussion. If I was going down, they were going with me!

We began with a mediocre topic – not too controversial, but strong enough to prove we were willing to go "where no one has gone before." After introducing the key players and announcing the topic, to our surprise we found that members were already sitting in opposing sections. How could that be? The topic was a secret! With eyebrows raised, I glanced at the Transition Team and continued coaching the ground rules with the congregation. I agreed to keep the process flowing smoothly, keep people on track, and keep discussions within established time limits. My personal commitment was to use coaching skills, provide a safe environment for everyone to share thoughts and feelings, and protect them from offensive comments. We would hear from everyone who wanted to speak.

To keep my promise, I needed a different set of listening skills. It required radar-like sensors to pay attention to what was *not being said* as well as to what was *implied* from numerous people simultaneously. I tried to play to the influential leaders and hoped that the less strong would grab on to that value. However, I still had to check in and make sure that everyone in the congregation received value. We clearly wrote the topic and goal of each session on a whiteboard at the front of the room. This helped everyone stay on task as a group. If the topic involved intricate details or statistics, the Transition Team prepared handouts. We often ended sessions by scheduling a special church-wide activity that would deal more specifically with the issue. We also used the whiteboard to outline a plan of action to ensure follow-up.

We watched as congregants stepped into different roles. Regardless of their church responsibilities, we made sure that no one dominated the conversation and that everyone heard and understood all who spoke. Brainstorming was a great tool in helping reluctant members speak up. The synergy generated in the room often drew them right into the discussion, and they were contributing before they realized it.

Here are some of the basic group coaching techniques and skills used throughout the sessions:

- Begin each session with prayer to allow the group to connect with their Christian beliefs and values in their behavior towards one another.
- Position other leaders near the coach to demonstrate a united front.
- Prepare the coach and other leaders mentally by anticipating any difficulties or biases that might emerge from past problems, issues, or concerns regarding possible topics.
- At each session, reach an agreement with the group on the common topic for the session.
- Create an environment for people to share without threats.
- Encourage the group to attack the issue, not the person.
- Be ready to defuse the slightest personal attack on anyone speaking, regardless of the content. Honor the value of each individual comment by asking someone other than the commenter to repeat the comment.
- If the group's focus becomes misdirected or distracted, stop and ask the group if they heard what the last speaker said. Again, ask someone to repeat or summarize what he or she heard.

- Challenge the group to reach solutions they have not considered previously. Only after they have exhausted what they know will they tap their creative nature and discover fresh new possibilities.
- Expect synergy to emerge out of new thoughts and ideas from the group.
- Assist those who struggle to find the right words by reflecting back the essence of their contribution. With permission, clarify the content by reframing or contextualizing any confusing dialogue.
- Ask the group or commenter to explain any cultural or historical comments (e.g. inside jokes, past situations) to allow everyone equal understanding. Create common strengths through exercises and activities that allow the group to accomplish something together.
- Do not automatically answer every question. When appropriate, create group ownership by having group members research the information and bring it back to the group.
- Provide handouts when sharing a volume of information to avoid redundancy and/or long, boring readings. Capture group memory by recording all contributions on a whiteboard or flip chart.
- Coach the group to choose the best solution and develop a plan of action for the topic discussed.
- Always make specific follow-up assignments for each group decision, including accountability for completion and deadlines.
- Finally, before leaving each session, confirm any group decision(s) by asking someone to read the action plan from the whiteboard or flip chart.

Members could not remember when they last felt so unified and involved. Many commented that they were learning about themselves as well as the church. Questions about other processes in the church began to surface with hopeful expectation. However, there were some who never got on board, stating, "This coaching is all silly talk. We need a pastor who is strong enough to just *tell us what to do!*"

Beyond the coaching tools and skills, it was imperative to remember that the focus was on the personal development of the one sharing with the group. One of the greatest joys of a coach is to see the synergy in the room support the individual as well. This does not always occur, but it is beautiful when it happens. Without this underlying focus, you will most likely end up with a train wreck.

Many times during the first session or two, I had to protect the speaker and even lovingly confront those who chose to attack a person rather than the issue. Even in confrontation, the coach must protect the delicate pride of the attacker. Asking the question, "What did you hear this person say?" would often deflect the emotion toward the facts and avoid a conflict. Another good clarifying question is, "Who can explain to us what this person just said?" Writing the essence of the statement on the whiteboard often reaffirms the individual and avoids having the same issue surface repeatedly. If someone else brings it up again, simply put a checkmark next to that line on the whiteboard and then ask, "What else?"

After several Sunday night sessions unfolded, I became more and more comfortable with our "Dialogue with the Pastor" program as we marched through fifty-one major issues. My fears eased as the congregation began to listen to each other and the many options that surfaced. They were learning that together they could come up with many more solutions than they could individually, and that it was okay to experiment with something new. This coaching approach helped me to realize that some members never expected anyone to resolve their favorite issue; they just wanted someone to hear their complaint.

A major breakthrough occurred one night that truly validated this coaching approach. We faced a vote at our next business meeting on a major issue that would affect the entire congregation. As one member was passionately sharing her thoughts, a person with an opposing view offered a crude remark. The person next to him gently said, "No, I want to hear what she is saying. That's a great idea!" At that very moment, you could hear a pin drop as everyone's gaze turned toward the person speaking and she gently said, "Thank you!" From that time forward, the entire congregation started protecting one another and really wanting to hear all sides of an issue. Suddenly they found themselves faced with the dilemma of how to make decisions with this new means of discussion and input from everyone! And that's another coaching story.

~~~~~~~~~~~~~~~~~~~~~~~~
~~~~~~~~~~~~~~~~~~~~~~~~

Ed Hale is a seasoned minister of thirty-six years and a full-time consultant and coach trainer for the Church Starting Department of the Texas Baptist Convention. He is currently attaining his professional certified coach (PCC) credential with the International Coach Federation. His passion is to train coaches for local churches, associations, and businesses across Texas. As an adjunct professor at Dallas Baptist University, he teaches a coaching concentration within several of the master-level degree programs. He also loves to coach and facilitate transition teams in pastorless churches that are committed to the Intentional Interim Program as they prepare for their next pastor.

Coaching's Contribution to Dream Fulfillment: Finding the Ultimate Ministry Setting

By Larry Ousley

"Your vision will become clear when you can look into your own heart. Who looks outside dreams; who looks inside awakens." – Carl Jung

"My life is better than my dreams," John reflected during our coaching session. As the pastor of an urban church in a multicultural, transitional community setting, he felt at home in living out his deep calling to ministry. The reality of his world of ministry in the northeastern United States fit him better – so much better than when he had felt "stuck" in what seemed like a dead-end setting in the rural south. What a journey it had been these last four years, but now he was home. He had awakened to his new, more fulfilling life and ministry.

John came to me because he was struggling in a ministry setting that in many ways seemed to be squelching him. He had hoped that his life in the ministry would be more fulfilling, and he was starting to fear that he would be stuck in this and future settings that squeezed the life out of him. Music symbolized it for him; he loved classical music, but he was living in a country music world.

It was probably hard for the bishop and cabinet to find the right placement for him as a liberal person in a conservative area of the rural south. John had told me as we began coaching that he felt like he was the most liberal person in his annual conference. His first appointments were in isolated, rural settings where he really felt stifled and like he could not be himself. His theological perspective was so far removed from his parishioners' that the gap was almost intolerable for him, but even more so for them!

When the possibility of being an associate pastor at a 1,000-member, county-seat United Methodist Church (UMC) came up, he thought that setting would be the best fit within the conference. He knew the senior pastor a bit and thought they could work together. However, after being there for a year, John was unhappy, including in his relationship with the senior pastor. He saw the senior pastor as extremely dictatorial towards him, as well as in his leadership of the congregation. It was during this time of desperation that his district superintendent referred John to me for coaching.

His district superintendent knew enough about coaching to realize that John might benefit from coaching, since he was not experiencing deep, interpersonal issues, but rather a lack of clarity about his dreams and how to achieve them. It wasn't so much that he needed "fixing," as that he needed to clarify his values and his calling, and then find ways to create a better congruence between his yearnings and his life and ministry. He knew that his current ministry setting and journey were not resonating with his deep values and the essence of who he was, both as a person and as the minister God was calling him to be.

Coaching Process

Over several months of coaching, we identified and clarified John's most significant values, greatest strengths, and deepest yearnings. While we began to dream up what a more appropriate setting would be like, we focused on the current reality: the poor health of his relationship with the senior pastor and his lack of fit with the culture of the church and the community in general. We identified at least three possible stages in moving from the present situation of unhappiness to a more blissful experience:

1. Making the most of the current setting

2. Seeking a different setting with a better fit – recognizing that this might be a stepping stone on the way to the *most* desirable setting

3. Securing the ministry location with the ultimate fit

1. Making the most of the current setting:

While I continued to coach John individually, I also brought in a certified relationship coach to work on the relationship between John and the senior pastor. This effort helped make the relationship more tolerable for John. The senior pastor and John both agreed that it would be best to end their partnership and John's placement at the church.

I continued to coach John individually during this stage. The first phase of our coaching focused on helping John catch a vision of what was possible as he moved toward his future in ministry, and helping him regain a sense of hope for a more fulfilling setting. We also explored the possibility that ministry might not be for him. As well, the coaching sessions helped him experience and express the depths of his frustration with and disappointment in his current situation.

Further, we found ways for John to find more enjoyment and fulfillment in the present by changing his perspective and developing more appreciation for how God was at work in the current situation. John was awakened to the good that was happening in his setting, and as he envisioned new possibilities on the horizon he could more readily appreciate the gifts in the present.

In coaching, we speak of helping our coachees develop their muscles. We don't lift the weights for them – we help train them for heavier lifting. John developed the skills of appreciating what is and finding joy and fulfillment in it, while at the same time looking forward to an even better fit in a new pastoral assignment.

2. Seeking a different setting with a better fit:

We used various processes for identifying ministry settings that might be more fulfilling for John, as he began to clarify the kind of setting to which he felt called. He realized that it might not be possible to move directly into just the right setting, since there might not be an opening there. Yet he knew he wanted to leave his current situation as soon as possible.

Thus, we strategized that John's journey to the "promised land" on the other side of the stream might require at least one stepping stone along the way. While initially that was a disappointing conclusion for him, he realized that securing the setting of his dreams would be worth the wait. And moving to a transitional setting would relieve much of the negativity he was experiencing now.

While John felt called in this stage of ministry to being a solo or senior pastor on the East Coast where he could be near his family, it worked out that he could move quicker by taking another associate position which was on the West Coast. He had gone to seminary on the West Coast and used some of his connections there to find an associate position in a large city in California.

During his three years in California at this in-between setting, John and I only spoke occasionally. In these coaching sessions, we reflected on his dream and how it was happening in that setting, and we continued to strategize about how John might reach an even more desirable ministry setting. Then, through networking within an urban ministry professional association, John discovered what appeared to be his dream situation.

3. <u>Securing the ministry location with the ultimate fit:</u>

After identifying the desired pastoral appointment to an urban ministry setting in the Northeast, John and I began to focus on how to communicate his wishes to the district superintendent of that area. John found that he was so drawn to the setting that he became anxious and was fearful that he would not be selected for it. Through coaching we addressed his inner critic and used role-play to rehearse his conversations with the district superintendent. In the end, he was able to authentically express his passion for urban ministry, and was selected for the position.

It was a privilege to be John's companion on the four-year journey from a "stuck" place to an energized place where he was living out his calling in a setting that allowed him to be himself and express some of the unique aspects of ministry to which he felt called.

Reflections

- Coaching is not primarily about solving problems. It's about helping people clarify and live out their dreams. However, people are often motivated to seek a coaching relationship because of some negative set of circumstances or challenges in their lives. And coaching does help coachees *build their own muscles* for dealing with the challenges and opportunities in their lives on an ongoing basis. Coaching empowers coachees to seek fulfillment, engagement, and depth in their lives.

- One of the dilemmas for new coaches can be where to begin. Early on, it is essential to create rapport with the coachee and design together a coaching agreement. Then you want to listen deeply to get some picture of the coachee's current reality and his or her reason for coming to coaching. Sometimes this involves processing emotions so that coachees are not caught in them and prevented from moving ahead. But as soon as you have done all this, it is paramount that you help awaken some degree of hope about their situation, including a vision of what is possible. This vision will provide the energy to do the work/play of building their new life.
- Coaching is about helping coachees live "at choice." Powerful questioning is a crucial tool for helping them see things differently. Powerful questions come with the expectation of choice and possibility. When we as coaches ask powerful questions, we stand in a place of hope and choice, and an opportunity for change. We are living in that assumption with the coachee and helping them move toward hope, choice, and change rather than remain stuck. There would be no purpose in asking powerful questions if there were not the possibility of new awareness and new perspectives leading toward transformative action. As coaches, we ground this assumption in our way of being as we hold the space and ask powerful questions. This is a Christian stance, for we have the promise that Christ makes "all things new." (Rev. 21:5)
- As a coach revealing the hope for choice and possibility for the coachee, I maintain that greater choice and fulfillment is *always possible,* even in our most frustrating situations. Further, people who are moving into greater choice based on their deep calling create a ripple effect for those around them. They raise the possibility that other people in their setting can also play a bigger game.
- Arnold Mindell's concept of three levels of reality informs my coaching and impacted my work with John. Mindell drew on

traditions of the Australian Aborigines, including their ideas about dreaming. The three levels are called essence, dreaming, and consensus reality. People live mostly in the third level, consensus reality, and John was stuck in a particular configuration of this reality. In order to help him awaken to himself and dream God's dream for him, we had to dive into the essence level to discover his and God's unique yearnings within him. Then we were able to use processes to focus on the dreaming level to envision possibilities and begin to explore concrete options in the world of consensus reality.

- People are often so overwhelmed by their immediate situation that they feel stuck and hopeless about anything changing – at least changing very much. In order to get unstuck, people need a compelling vision that draws them forward to a preferred future. The inertia of the immediate situation tends to hold one in place by homeostatic forces. However, once the movement begins toward a compelling vision, one begins to gain momentum – especially with the help of a supportive partner such as a coach. However, merely feeling unhappy in one's present situation does not provide the leverage to get out of the mire of paralysis. The difference between a river and a swamp is that in a swamp, the water just pools, becomes immobile, and stinks. The river, on the other hand, is flowing toward its yearning within structures (banks) it has created. Coaching provides a lifeline to help people pull themselves out of the muck, catch a vision of where they want to head, and build the channels that allow them to flow with ease, enjoyment, and fulfillment into new, more blissful lives. In this wonderful life God has given us, there is no reason not to live in bliss and resonance, even in difficult situations.

Applications

- *If you are a coach*, I have two invitations: 1) Celebrate the opportunities you have to help people create bigger and richer lives than they are presently living. You are their companion on the journey to fully live the life and the calling that our wonderful Creator gifts them toward. The more people who are flourishing in this God-resonant life, the more fully and the quickly God's realm will be expressed among all God's creatures. 2) How might you open more fully to the yearnings of God within you? Do you have a coach to partner with you toward your own bigger and richer life?

- *If you are not a coach*, I also have two invitations. 1) Spend some time reflecting on your life. To what degree are you living a life of flow, in sync with God and your deepest self, flourishing in your God-given purpose? Celebrate the degree to which this is happening. Commit yourself to doing whatever it takes to live in the rhythm and balance of being and doing what you are called to. 2) If you don't have a coach, consider hiring one. All great players have coaches!

"Go confidently in the direction of your dreams. Live the life you've imagined!" – Thoreau

~~~~~~~~~~~~~~~~~~~~~~~~~

Dr. Larry Ousley (Larry@LarryOusley.com) is the executive director of the Intentional Growth Center (IGC). Before coming to IGC in 2000, he served as senior pastor of several large churches. He is a professional certified coach (PCC) through the International Coach Federation. Larry is also an endorsed life coach through the United Methodist Endorsing Agency, a certified organizational relationship systems coach (ORSCC) and a faculty member at Coaching4Clergy. You can visit his website at www.LarryOusley.com.
~~~~~~~~~~~~~~~~~~~~~~~~~

Focus Coaching: Empowering Clergy with Focus, Even When the Earth Quakes

By Sue Politte

Being in an earthquake is an odd and disorienting experience. At first you sense something weird, and then you hear the rattling. You feel off balance before you realize the whole world is shaking. Thoughts race uncontrollably through your mind. Where is a safe place? You totally lose focus on what you were doing; the crisis interrupts your focus. For many of my coachees, unwanted shifts in focus are common and bring on a myriad of challenges.

Focus coaching attracts two main groups of people. Both groups experience similar challenges of distractions, feeling overwhelmed, disorganization, and forgetfulness. They realize that this lack of focus is clearly a roadblock keeping them from accomplishing what they've set out to do.

One group is made up of the ADHD types who've always had difficulty with focusing. Over time they may have acquired skills and tools to manage these challenges, but those skills and tools may have stopped working for them. Sometimes this happens when they experience major changes, such as growth in their ministry.

The people in the second group have also experienced some sort of major change – a life earthquake, complete with aftershocks. Their world is quaking, so their ability to focus is shot. The quaking constantly redirects their thoughts, wrecks their organizational abilities, and causes forgetfulness.

All of us are subject to earthquakes in life, even those in ministry. The following story shows how focus coaching can clear a path forward that may have been blocked for years, and help in many other ways as well.

In an instant, Bob's eyes said it all. The ministry leader sitting across from me was not my typical, busy, ADHD clergy coachee wanting to get rid of distractions, boost his effectiveness, or actually see his vision become reality while finding fulfillment in the journey. These eyes held pain, apprehension, and frustration. Bob's shoulders had slumped. His energy was gone. All this happened after I simply asked how things had gone since our last session – his second.

Bob looked me in the eye and said, "I wasn't able to complete my action steps and I'm ready to tell you why." It had started quite a while back, when his precious daughter was attacked in a heartbreaking random act of violence. Bob's family earthquake had just begun. Aftershocks included gut-wrenching changes in his daughter as she struggled unsuccessfully to deal with what had happened. For the first time ever, there were massive behavioral issues. Bob and his wife were doing everything they could, spending much time, energy, and money trying to help their daughter. Nothing worked. She continued on a downward spiral. Bob's ministry focus and normal activities were constantly interrupted by these aftershocks – thoughts and concerns, phone calls from the school, appointments with counselors and doctors, etc. This was on top of Bob's already busy schedule, people arriving to see him unannounced, and increasing requests from people needing help from the ministry.

I inquired about Bob's visits with counselors and doctors. Sadly, one of the many counselors actually placed blame on Bob, saying God was punishing Bob for how he had been as a teen. I saw the deep pain that caused. I asked him, "What do you think God would say about that?" "Absurd," was the answer. "God forgave me completely years ago." Bob was actually in ministry to reach people who were where he had once been. I reminded him of what a truly wonderful ministry he led and how many people's lives had been changed by the love and care shown them in Jesus's name. A flash of faith came through as he dared to hope, "Maybe somehow God will turn this all around for good."

But the hope faded as he explained that although he had prayed, sought God's direction, and involved multiple experts, still the destructive aftershocks continued. Bob blasted, "I've been doing everything. I'm at the end of my rope. Where is God? Is this some kind of sick joke? I'm holding on as hard as I can. I don't know how long I can hold on, hoping that God will come through." Bob paused, seeming somewhat shocked by what he'd said.

A simple question came to my mind. "Bob," I asked, "what would happen if you let go?" It was as if all the air had been sucked out of the room. Bob's shoulders went back and I could see him rapidly processing internally. I was blessed to witness how God's presence in Bob lifted his head and unlocked the false and binding stronghold. He declared, "If I let go, I'd find myself sitting in God's hands." Bob continued, telling how awesome and powerful God is, how wonderful the gift of salvation and new life that Jesus gives is, complete with love and hope. Looking back, this is the point that Bob and I both see as the major turning point.

The next week, the new Bob was ready to tackle his challenges with scheduling and distractions that pop up during the day. He told me, "I really want an open-door policy, but I can't get everything done and still talk to everybody." Over the next few weeks of coaching, he developed ways to schedule his life so it would work for his situation. We worked on building healthy boundaries. We found time for Bob to connect with family and friends. At work, he focused on connecting with those who would most benefit the ministry's vision. He put the task "Report to Sue" (that's me) on his calendar, feeling that this accountability would help him develop these new skills. He also scheduled time for himself and for connecting with God.

Bob arrived at one of his coaching appointments concerned about how others might see his organizational system – stacks and piles – possibly as a sign that he was not being effective or was not capable of organizing himself. We explored and affirmed that it was *how Bob needed the space around him to work* that was important. We also incorporated his concerns about how his office appeared. Another discovery was that he needed to have his schedule and information with him on-the-go, and for that we employed technology. He realized he had falsely assumed that he had to organize in the same ways that other people do. Instead, we developed several structures that worked for Bob. He began to regularly make it to meetings on time, along with whatever materials he needed. He soon reported,

"My stress is down, I can find stuff, and I'm getting more done!" In the midst of his aftershocks, he had connected deeply with his God – his solid foundation. Through coaching, he developed and implemented strategies that kept him focused on what was important.

When Bob shared that he noticed another staff member having similar frustrations with focus and lateness, I shared how focus issues – ADHD or not – are very common in the ministry. He realized that coaching would be a benefit for this staff member, *and* he realized he could do some seeding immediately. In a coaching session, he decided to seed by example and directions. In meetings he would say things like, "Let's all get that on our calendars now," and "Everybody write this down on your to-do list for next week." He would joke, "Everybody has a to-do tab or notebook so you won't lose your lists, right?" Bob realized that customizing his focus strategies through coaching had served him very well. He also knew that tossing out simple ideas and examples was a good start in helping his staff to become empowered and effective, too.

Over the next few months, Bob and I met regularly for coaching sessions. His staff noticed his progress and wondered how coaching could help them. He had me work with his staff around managing their increasing requests for ministry services.

Coaching had quite an impact on Bob's life and his ministry. While the earth still quaked, Bob's search to gain and keep focus brought structures, boundaries, and awareness that empowered him and others to reach for an even bigger vision.

The last time we talked, Bob was excited. He wanted to update me and tell me how our coaching had helped open a new door. The quaking had stopped. Bob's precious daughter had completed a major turnaround. She has talked publicly about her experiences and God's faithfulness. Bob said that his new skills had also allowed him to move into a larger ministry role that would impact many more people. Having experienced how a coaching approach can help unlock the door for God to enter into a situation, Bob was working to implement a coaching approach himself. As we said our goodbyes, Bob said, "Remember how I wondered if God would somehow turn this around for good? Look what He did. It's more than I had ever imagined."

As someone with ministry involvement but no formal ministry training, here are some of the things I have discovered as I've partnered with my clergy and ministry coachees:

God has equipped our coachees. The truth is already inside them. Coaching in a ministry setting is powerful. Massive power lies inside our coachees as they choose to tap in to their true source of strength and their God-given gifts and talents. It's about alignment. Coaching can unlock false beliefs and limiting assumptions. Our coachees are the ones who seize the truth and become free.

Powerful questions are just waiting inside our coachees. Questions are keys to unlocking potential and what God is up to, here and now. The most powerful questions are the simplest, formed from the depths of what our coachees are telling us. They are the dare-to-ask, catalyst questions. "What would happen if you let go?" removed the barrier that had separated Bob from his strong foundation, his God. He became ready to fight the good fight and overcome. And he has.

Attending to your own personal foundation equips you for co-creating and guarding the safe coaching place for the coachee. Respect the process God is bringing the coachee through. I've found it necessary to be anchored to my foundational rock. Having this anchor enabled me to ask and accompany Bob as he faced the question he had not been able to look at himself, "What if...?"

It's all about customizing. What will work for your coachee? Focus coaching develops ways to reduce distractions by implementing personalized planning and organizational strategies, along with healthy boundaries.

The power of accountability and encouragement significantly increases results for your focus coachees. Listen to what each individual needs to help them accomplish their goals. Celebrate their successes *and* their efforts. Celebrate what God is doing in and through them!

Enjoy your focus coachees – they are an inspiration and a joy.

~~~~~~~~~~~~~~~~~~~~~~~~~~
~~~~~~~~~~~~~~~~~~~~~~~~~~

Sue Politte is a focus coach, empowering and supporting those with adult ADHD or other focus challenges to win battles with distractions, disorganization, and/or feelings of being overwhelmed. Her coachees experience increased effectiveness and productivity, and find support for their next level of fulfilling success/vision. Sue also provides workshops such as Life-Long Strategies for Success. Sue is the president of Success In Focus LLC, where she coaches and supports coachees. As Coaching4Clergy faculty, she trains coaches. Please visit www.SuccessInFocusLLC.com.

Proverbs 29:18

If people can't see what God is doing, they stumble all over themselves; but when they attend to what God reveals, they are most blessed.

SECTION FOUR:

Creating a Larger Coaching Culture

So far in this anthology we have addressed coaching and coach training for the individual, team, and local church. This section addresses the larger groups – associations, conferences, and jurisdictions – and how these larger groups can benefit from a coaching approach to ministry.

More and more ministry groups are discovering the difference that coaching can make. From clergy effectiveness and review, to clarity of vision and coaching upward, a coaching approach matters.

How to Create a Coaching Culture in Your Conference, Association, or Local Church

By J. Val Hastings

Ministry leaders regularly approach me about creating a coaching culture in their conference, association, or local church. They are usually the primary decision-makers in their organizations, and are in a position to impact the larger organization.

Most of these individuals represent organizations that are either in recline or just beginning to decline. They are looking for resources and tools to turn things around. They've either had personal experience with being coached, or they've seen the benefits of coaching with select individuals in their organization. They're already sold on coaching and coach training.

The challenge is to create a coaching culture without having it viewed by their constituency as the latest fad or top-down directive that they *must* participate in. They want this to be an organic experience, and they want their members to buy-in to the coaching culture.

Aside from having experienced coaching, these ministry leaders have usually asked around to find out how other organizations have implemented coaching (though in the past there have been very few successful models or practitioners to ask). What has worked? What is still working? Through word-of-mouth, along with our coaching training events, they found their way to my company, Coaching4Clergy.

From there, core members of the association, conference, or local church participated in our Accelerated Coach Training. This gave them a thorough understanding of coaching and specific coaching skills and techniques. The training includes a mentor-coaching component (either individually or as a group), through which they not only honed their coaching skills but also developed an implementation plan for creating a coaching culture.

Every implementation plan included the following elements:

- Ministry leaders sent personal invitations to the members of their organization, as well as mass invitations and informational flyers.
- They held open coaching demonstrations.
- They did not try to apply a cookie-cutter culture, but allowed the new culture to form organically.
- They listened to their members and actually coached their organization into a new culture.
- They raised funds so that the cost of coaching and coach training did not stop their efforts.
- They recognized that coaching isn't the answer to everything; coaching is part of the answer, which also includes therapy, consulting, and other skill sets.
- They were realistic about time; things weren't going to change overnight.
- Every one of these ministry leaders also became a coach trainer.
- Each of the ministry leaders was personally convinced of the value of coaching and the difference it could make in their organization.

The ministry leaders I have worked with have experienced tremendous benefits from their efforts to create coaching cultures in their organizations. In one conference, every newly appointed pastor was assigned a coach. In addition, a coach was assigned to work with the board of any church that was receiving a new pastor – typically a time when conflicts surface. This program is now in its fourth year, and the coaches in place have been able to assist numerous churches and pastors in a healthy, constructive approach to conflict.

One conference developed a catchy slogan: *"Every pastor has a coach and is a coach."* At least that's the goal. Currently 40 percent of the member pastors have received basic coach training and are now practicing in pairs and triads with other pastors who have the same level of skill. Most are meeting once a month; in some cases, more frequently. The ministry leaders in this association have noted a definite increase in clergy morale. They are also noticing heightened interest from pastors outside of their association, attracted to their churches mainly because of this coaching culture.

In another association, the majority of pastors have now received the benefits of coaching and coach training. They are using these skills in their local communities and outreach opportunities. For example, several pastors have worked together with volunteer police chaplains to bring coaching to police and their work in the community. Other pastors have offered coach training to neighborhood non-profit organizations.

I asked two of the leaders from the Tarrant Baptist Association what suggestions they would offer a ministry leader looking to create a coaching culture in his or her association, conference, or local church. Becky Biser, Director of Leadership Development, suggests:

- Incorporate coaching into everything you are doing to create the culture, including all staff meetings, committee and team meetings, small groups, and Bible studies. When you receive guests or have scheduled appointments, use the coach approach with them as well. It has to become *your* culture for it to transfer into your church, conference, or association.
- Invest in key leaders and influencers by providing free coaching and coach training. They will be some of your best advocates for moving the culture forward.
- Use coaching questions in all your communications. You have to be totally invested in order for the culture to spread.

Gary Crowell, the association's chief financial officer, had this to add:

- Seek to establish some real-life success stories about how coaching has benefitted them, individually and as congregations.
- Invest your most sustained coach-training efforts on those who surface as the "hot hearts" for developing coaching skills, rather than in dispersed blasts that find little fertile ground.

- Talk the walk. Continually tell your audience how coaching is a powerful tool that results in tangible positive change (announcements, print, e-mail, web, video, etc.).
- Model coaching constantly in multiple venues within the ministry setting to effectively show how it works.
- Keep improving and refining your own skills as a coach through reading and practice. The best leaders know their subject well and know how to transfer it convincingly to others.

~~~~~~~~~~~~~~~~~~~~~~~~~

J. Val Hastings, MCC, is the founder and president of Coaching4Clergy, which provides specialized training for pastors, church leaders, and coaches. Val hired his first coach while he was pastoring at a local United Methodist church. His progress was noticed by all, and he began to wonder, "What if I adopted a coaching approach to ministry? What if the larger church adopted a coaching approach to ministry?" In that moment a vision began to emerge – a global vision: *Every pastor, ministry staff, and church leader a coach.*

Val is the author of *The Next Great Awakening: How to Empower God's People with a Coach Approach to Ministry,* and the e-book, *The E3-Church: Empowered, Effective and Entrepreneurial Leadership That Will Keep Your Church Alive.* Val currently holds the designation of master certified coach through the International Coach Federation, the highest coaching designation.
~~~~~~~~~~~~~~~~~~~~~~~~~

Coaching from First Chair: Leading Using Coaching

By David Biser

The look of ministry has changed dramatically in the last twenty years. Ministry staffs, congregations, and pastors have sought new techniques as they have seen the need for revitalization in the local church. These new opportunities in leadership styles, offered by authors both inside and outside of the church community, have sparked exciting new possibilities. Outdated styles of leadership are fast being replaced by methods that value individual learning styles and look at each individual as gifted and blessed by God. Coupled with tools like spiritual gift inventories, strengths assessments (e.g. StrengthsFinder), and personality tests (e.g. DISC, Myers-Briggs), pastoral leaders are newly equipped to lead both congregations and staff in powerful and positive directions.

Over the last five years I have come to place a high value on coaching as a leadership style. The previous styles of leadership that I learned have become obsolete. My training in the U.S. Marine Corps, for example, taught me to lead by example, accompanied by a significant amount of yelling and physical punishment. The corporate model taught me to lead by direction: *I will tell you what to do and you will do it.* My family model was filled with: *Do as I say, not as I do.* Those models of leadership will only get the pastoral leader so far, as they each contain built-in ceilings that impose limits on what can be accomplished. The great advantage of a coaching model for pastoral leadership is the immense value it places on the individual as a whole person working in tandem with the greater staff and congregation. In this system, the leader views each person as an individual as well as part of the whole, and considers the forces at work in all directions.

At CrossPoint Church, we have incorporated a coaching leadership style across the board for all staff members, mandating coach training for each member of our core staff – those people at the top of the organizational chart. Many went on to take extra coach training, beyond what was required. There is not a day that goes by in our office without a coaching question being asked of one person to another. These questions are used to enhance our ability to work together as a team, to achieve the desired outcome for a specific ministry, and to ultimately see the mission and vision of the entire church realized.

Leading Using Coaching

Coaching has helped our team members move into important conversations about their ministry and the ministry of their fellow staff members. Difficult conversations have been made easier via a non-threatening coaching method that encourages each person to reach for what God has in store for their ministry, the church, and themselves. As the senior pastor on staff, I have watched team members coaching each other toward new observations and possibilities with questions that draw out the heart and desires of the individual. Team members have been able to make key observations about each other and raise them in non-threatening ways. Sometimes I have heard, "Quit coaching me!" accompanied by a lot of laugher, when someone had suddenly realized that he or she was being coached. That being said, each person on the vision team values the time, energy, and thought of their fellow team members, and feels appreciated when another team member takes the time to offer coaching.

The two outcomes of 1) more open conversations, and 2) more sharing of observations, would have been enough to convince me that the hard work of shifting to a coaching leadership style is worth it. But there are even more great effects of coaching for leaders. This model of ministry leadership has allowed us to look for godly direction in the personal and vocational lives of our team members as well as in specific ministry areas. Team members have asked directional questions that have allowed the person being coached to move into a place of new discovery. We've seen coaching open doors for people that we never dreamed of – doors to themselves and to the ministry they are leading. Some people have gone on personal and spiritual retreats; others have adjusted their ministry focus.

Coaching into New Adventures

One of the wonderful opportunities that coaching has brought to our team members is when new futures become visible to the person being coached. Many times I've seen ministry leaders so wrapped up in their current ministry responsibilities that they are unable to see what great opportunities are right in front of them. Often this only takes a short conversation with pointed coaching questions that allow the team member to take a step back from the chaos of the moment and see what God is placing right in front of his or her eyes. Those coaching questions are different for each team member and situation, but I can tell you that a few have opened exciting new doors for our staff. These coaching opportunities are often at their highest when other changes are taking place in the organization. Any change – whether it is a change of pastor, worship times or styles, or physical surroundings – can be a catalyst for discovering new adventures for the future.

Through the key practices of coaching I have witnessed several staff members and ministry servants make lateral moves from one ministry to another. The wonderful thing about serving in the Kingdom is that there are both lifetime callings and seasonal callings. A lifetime calling might be to a local congregation, pastoral ministry, or the mission field. A seasonal calling may result in a youth leader becoming a campus pastor, a children's pastor moving into senior adult ministries, or a campus pastor becoming a lead pastor. Coaching allows a leader who is sensing a seasonal change to process his or her feelings and the sense of God's directional tug. Coaching also reduces surprises by allowing the leader to identify thoughts and trends that might lead to future changes.

Coaching can also facilitate a person's move out of a ministry. There are times in every church and organization when someone should move over, move on, or move out. Coaching values the person and looks for the next opportunity that individual can move into. Coaching also strives to help that individual find the future paths that are right in front of them, waiting for them to step upon. We have been able to do this several times at CrossPoint. One full-time youth pastor moved into a campus pastor position and then moved out from CrossPoint to a new opportunity in teaching that he was feeling a call to pursue. We remain friends, and it was one of the best moves we all could have made. Everyone is happy. And while that kind of success story does not happen every time, when it does it makes coaching worth more than its weight in gold.

In a similar situation, we had hired a new youth pastor who was also tasked with being the worship leader for a blended worship service. During his interview I let him know that if he came to work for us we would be in a state of constant dialogue (coaching). I told him these conversations would be our way of making sure he was happy and fulfilled. They would also be ways for us to move him out or away from a ministry or into a new area of serving if he felt God calling him in a different direction. Within a year we realized that this youth pastor should be a part of our contemporary service and not our blended service. We had a round peg we were trying to fit into a square hole, and it was not working for anyone. Coaching provided the setting to have a conversation in which he was comfortable stating how he was feeling, and I was comfortable as well. We were able to identify the issues and concerns, label the needed changes, and establish a timeline for change; coaching gave us the format for a non-threatening conversation in which we could all look forward to a win/win result.

As the vision pastor and senior leader at CrossPoint Church, nothing makes me happier and more satisfied than when I see a fellow leader/servant find their groove for ministry. Through coaching, our team has been able to help each other see our current levels of effectiveness as well as new ministries that may be on the horizon. When the proverbial light bulb turns on for a person during coaching, there is an excitement for both coach and coachee. That ongoing excitement encourages us to dream out loud, process openly with each other, and share ideas and possibilities with enthusiasm rather than fear.

Coaching out the Door

There are those times when coaching reveals what no one wants to see. Problems that have been kept quiet or hidden can be exposed during a coaching interaction. Sometimes there are differences in thought, mission, vision, theology, methodology, or philosophy that mean a team member needs to be coached out the door. Luckily, coaching also provides opportunities to deal with those concerns so that a healthy resolution can be found.

The first responsibility of the leader is to the God-given mission and vision of the organization. If, through coaching, the leader discovers a person who is serving in a key area but is not on board with the mission/vision or is simply not the right person for the team, it is the leader's obligation to try to coach that servant out the door and into some other area of work or ministry in which they can be effective. Note that there will also be times when coaching can take a person to the edge, but the leader must make the final call about the future of the person's employment. While this can be uncomfortable, in the long run coaching a person out the door can be the best thing for the organization and everyone involved.

~~~~~~~~~~~~~~~~~~~~~~~~~

David Biser is the vision pastor of CrossPoint Church, a multi-site church with three campuses in the greater Harrisburg, Pennsylvania, area. Dave has been in full-time ministry for twenty-three years and has been at CrossPoint for fifteen years. He is a graduate of Messiah College and Eastern Seminary. He has led his congregation through massive changes that moved them from traditional to modern, from single- to multi-site, and from inwardly focused to missional. Dave has been married to Julie for thirty years and has three adult children.
~~~~~~~~~~~~~~~~~~~~~~~~~

Building the Bridge as We Walk on It: Coaching in a United Methodist Conference

By David P. Hyatt

"I just want to help our churches reach out to the mission fields in their communities," Reverend Bob Farr spoke up. "We have to do something to help pastors become better leaders to reach people for Christ."

"Let's put together a process for training pastors; we could read books on leadership, get together monthly to share our learnings, and add some coaching to bring it all back home," I added.

"That's what they do in our school system to really develop their teachers and staff. Do you think we could do this in the church?" asked Bob.

"I can get some pastors to sign up. We have plenty of churches that are declining, and the pastors often aren't sure what to do," suggested Reverend Phil Neimeyer.

The Healthy Church Initiative in the Missouri Conference of the United Methodist Church was born out of this conversation I had in the spring of 2005 with Pastor Bob Farr of Church of the Shepherd, and Gateway Regional District Superintendent Phil Neimeyer. We began to build the bridge to our communities and neighborhood mission fields. We put together an eight-month course called Pastoral Leadership Development (PLD) and launched it in the fall of 2005, with twelve pastors in the four-hour class that Bob taught at his church. I was the administrator and "set-up guy," and coached all the pastors on their personal and ministry issues. Bob developed the outlines for the classes, and we also chose one leadership book per month for the pastors to read.

The following year brought fourteen more pastors who were eager to learn and responded to Phil's invitation to join this new process that would be helpful to them and their churches. We continued the coaching since we saw the benefit for each pastor in working on personal and local issues integrating what they were learning from the class sessions.

Another addition in 2006 was to gather together six pastors to form a type of mastermind group. Some were in the PLD class, some were not. This group, known affectionately as the Six Pack, discussed the broader issues of what we could do to grow and develop our churches in the PLD class as well as other churches across the conference. We met monthly, reading a few leadership books and having some good informal discussions. I also coached each pastor in this group on their personal and ministry issues.

In the spring of 2007, we discovered Dr. Paul Borden through reading his book *Hit the Bullseye*. We asked Paul to come and talk with our Six Pack and we were mesmerized as he laid out his "principles of transformation" and the process they had used in the American Baptist churches in Northern California. We were especially interested to learn how he credited coaching as key in the success of the transformation of their churches.

"We can do that," several said after listening to Paul. "Yes, but how?" others asked. We caught a vision and wondered how God could help us continue to help our churches reach the mission field to "make new disciples of Jesus Christ." How could we continue to build this bridge to our mission fields?

At this time, our bishop, Robert Schnase, had his eye on Bob Farr to help churches around the conference, since Bob had grown churches and was now developing this leadership process in St. Louis. Bishop Schnase appointed Bob to join the conference staff even as he continued to pastor Church of the Shepherd and transition this ministry to a new lead pastor. For a full year he did both jobs, and it almost killed him!

Bob's vision to help churches reach the mission field continued to grow as we took the Pastoral Leadership Development course to other districts around the Missouri Conference. This was the third year for PLD classes, and we did nine classes around the state with over 100 pastors participating. Since we believed every pastor needed a coach, I lined up as many coaches as we could find, using some professional coaches and some local church pastors.

When we met with Dr. Paul Borden, he emphasized that we would not change our churches with classes and seminars for the pastors. So in the fall of 2007, we took the next step. As a follow-up for the pastors who attended our training, we began offering weekend-long consultations at their churches. At the end of the weekend we would give five prescriptions to the church. If the church approved the implementation of the prescriptions, the pastor and church leaders would be coached for eighteen months to fulfill all five prescriptions. For this we needed coaches who would use *directive coaching* as we helped the churches fulfill the prescriptions they received on their consultation weekends.

After this first year of consultations, we added the Mystery Guest program developed by Faith Perceptions of Cape Girardeau. This process brought twelve guests from the community into each church to experience a Sunday morning. Each guest would fill out a questionnaire, and we used a composite report about the visits to help us know what Sunday morning was really like. This report proved to be extremely helpful to our team in developing the prescriptions for each church.

Here is the experience of one of the pastors who was coached through the prescription process following his church's consultation:

"The coaching process allowed for me to have a person looking at the 'big picture' with me on this journey. My coach was always asking me 'why' questions and prodding me to think about end results. Rather than offering me a lot of suggestions or solutions, I was encouraged to think creatively, and to think about how my actions and the actions of the church would contribute to 'making disciples.' I was stretched, encouraged to succeed, and given positive reinforcement when each goal was achieved." – Rev. Scott Bailey-Kirk, Pastor, Harrisonville UMC, Harrisonville, Missouri

At this point we had two kinds of coaching in effect across the Missouri Conference. The PLD courses were still using *supportive coaching* – six sessions for each pastor during the eight-month course.

One pastor gave his impressions of the coaching process:

"The coaching I have received in the PLD process is entirely different than the coaching I received in athletics. In athletics, the coach would tell us exactly what to do and this is the result that should occur. There was no room for discussion. However, in the PLD environment, the coaching was more flexible. It did not take long to understand that we already had the knowledge and the answers within us. The tools had already been provided through education, experience, and observation. It was a matter of bringing them out and putting them into practice. It has been a very rewarding experience and has impacted my ministry greatly." – Rev. Jerry Mattson, Williamsville/Greenville Charge, SE Missouri District

The second coaching process was the *directive approach*, intended to carry out the agenda of the prescriptions. The coach would walk with the pastor and the church for eighteen months following the approval of the prescriptions. We learned that the coaching was tremendously helpful to the actual fulfillment of the actions that were prescribed and the new behaviors that were being asked of the pastors and church leaders. It was especially important for the coaches to be on site to meet in person with the pastor and leaders, at least for the first six to eight months.

One coach had this to say about the support he received:

"Coaching has been and continues to be invaluable in my ministry. Through coaching I received a level of support and a level of challenge that no other process within the connection of United Methodism afforded me. My coaches helped me to stay at the 'balcony level' of viewing our ministry. By the same token, coaching kept my aim from being vague. Coaches held me accountable to specific goals and specific steps toward those goals. My coaches offered me more questions than directives, but their probing always got me toward traction in any given direction. Turning a church from inward focus and maintenance toward outward focus and disciple-making would be a lonely and/or impossible task without the consistent presence of effective coaching." – Rev. Geoff Posegate, First UMC, Sikeston, Missouri

By the fall of 2009, we had adopted a new curriculum for all our classes, developed by Ken Willard and Bob Farr. Now we were teaching the same missional principles and practices around the entire conference. By now, coaching had become an expected and needed part of the process of transforming our churches.

Bob Farr identifies the key reasons for using coaching:

1. We need someone to walk along with the pastor in the transforming process. Jesus never sent people out alone.

2. Lyle Schaller used to say that 90 percent of transformation efforts fail without a coach. We are seeing most of our churches being transformed in some way, some more than others.

3. Dr. Paul Borden taught us that a coach can say things the pastor can't. Often the pastor has been saying these things, but now the leaders are hearing it more effectively from the coach. The coach can take hits for the pastor as a kind of heat shield.

By 2011 we had about twenty coaches and we were coaching over 200 pastors. Some worked with many pastors and churches, others only a few. As the coach coordinator for both processes, I found that it was easier to manage a smaller number of coaches. As the coaches joined the project, we gave them some training and asked them to report to me about their sessions with their pastors and their churches. This system helped us develop new coaches each year so that we were able to use our experiences to continue to grow. As we refined all of our processes, especially coaching, we continued to build a bridge to the mission field.

In the summer of 2010, Reverend Karen Hayden joined the Missouri Conference staff to head up the Office of Pastoral Excellence. Karen added an important emphasis on coaching for all pastors and developed the Healthy Church Initiative for college ministries that, of course, included coaching. Karen was instrumental in helping us bring J. Val Hastings to Missouri to deliver his one-day Basic Coach Training in May of 2012, and in the future we will require all of our coaches to have this important training.

The Healthy Church Initiative continued to grow as we developed the Small Church Initiative (SCI) for churches with eighty and under in worship through the leadership of Kay Kotan, a credentialed coach with the International Coach Federation (ICF). The SCI provided a year-long joint training program for laity and pastors from several different churches. At the end of the year, each church had the opportunity for a one-day consultation and a follow-up process that included coaching. Coaching was not part of the year-long training, mostly for economic and practical reasons, but we have suggested to other conferences that coaching be part of this process, if possible.

A process for training laity called Lay Leadership Development (LLD) has been used for the past three years in our conference to parallel the PLD learning process for pastors. We have not used coaching yet in this course, but we may integrate it in the next year or so.

In our seventh year of changing and growing our churches in the Missouri Conference, we have so many blessings to share along the journey.

"I've had a coach for about five years. In that time we've talked about how to fire a staff person and how to leave an appointment well, how to create a staff team and how to live into an empty nest, how to prioritize and how to claim my own authority, and everything in between. My coach has asked probing questions and listened, reflected, and challenged – and all of that has formed my ministry into something more fruitful. I'm thankful for the monthly hour that is all about what I need to talk about." – Rev. Lynn Dyke, Mid State District Superintendent

Coaching has become one of our five key strategies for transforming our churches in the Missouri Conference. We have grown our process by raising the bar each year for our coaches, churches, and pastors, guided by the mission "to make new disciples of Jesus Christ for the transformation of the world." We are building bridges to our mission fields, but we know that is only half the calling; the other half is to walk across that bridge and engage people with Jesus Christ. Coaching helps greatly in developing churches with outward focus and connection with the community.

It's been an interesting seven-year journey since that conversation with Bob and Phil, wondering how we could help our churches build bridges to our neighborhood mission fields. The numbers share some of the good news. We have consulted in over 100 churches to move them forward in mission. We have trained over 400 pastors and about as many lay leaders in doing ministry in the twenty-first century. We have grown our processes each year and improved them to maximize our resources. Our conference showed growth in worship attendance two out of the last five years (that has only happened two other times between 1968 and 2008). We are also training some other conferences to build bridges to their communities through the Healthy Church Initiative.

One pastor shared the value of coaching for him: "I have found two significant advantages to having a coach. First it is someone to help me prioritize and plan my time, and help strategize with as well. A coach is most helpful with time management and keeping me on track to accomplish what I really want to get done. It helps keep the important, important. Second, to have a person you can share with in rough times that is not tied to your church and its system in any way, is an absolute joy. I remember one particular occasion when I had just had a horrible meeting and my coach helped me sort through that and see things from a different and fresh prospective." – Rev. Michael Blacksher, Asbury UMC, Springfield, Missouri

In all that we have done over these seven years, we have worked hard to be true to our mission to make new disciples of Jesus Christ for the transformation of the world. We feel very blessed and hope we have been a blessing to many people. It's never easy, but we know the Lord is with us as we "build the bridge as we walk on it." Thanks be to God!

~~~~~~~~~~~~~~~~~~~~~~~~

Dr. David P. Hyatt helped to create the Healthy Church Initiative in the Missouri Conference of the United Methodist Church, specifically overseeing the coaching. David was a pastor for twenty-six years in the Christian Church (Disciples of Christ), and has been coaching and consulting since 2001. He is a certified Christian leadership coach. For further information on the Healthy Church Initiative or the role of coaching in a judicatory or denominational setting, contact David at david@effectiveleadershipunlimited.com, by phone at 636-236-4488, or check out www.healthychurchinitiative.com.
~~~~~~~~~~~~~~~~~~~~~~~~

The Long Game: Incorporating Coaching into Ministry and Mentoring

By Claire Pedrick

In London, there are many areas like Grosvenor Square, the site of the US Embassy. This is the London of coffee table books, with streets full of enormous and beautiful old buildings. Many of these streets are owned by aristocratic family trusts with a long-term view of property management. If they want to buy back a building and fail to get it at auction, they just wait for forty years and try again the next time it is for sale. They understand that they are in the property market for the long game, and plan accordingly.

The Christian Church is in the faith business for the long game, but I sometimes wonder whether we forget to plan and develop accordingly. Our ministry is part of something that goes back to the first disciples, and will carry on until Jesus returns. We are part of God's big story – yet I wonder whether we pay enough attention to the emergent and changing world. In the UK, the context in which the church is ministering in the twenty-first century is significantly different than even thirty years ago. Ministers need all the internal formation that they have always needed – as well as some new skills, ideas, and support in leading in a very different society.

Jesus's style was to use a coaching approach. He did what he did and his disciples saw and asked questions. They would go off to quiet places to talk, to understand scripture, and to pray – even if that didn't always go to plan. (That probably sounds familiar!) And then they went off and did ministry and came back and talked about what had happened. What might it have looked like to see the disciples twenty years later? Like our churches today, they would have been encountering new and different contexts and would have had to reflect and prayerfully consider how to adapt.

The Very Reverend John Richardson is a priest who uses a coaching approach for the long game in order to support and develop his entrepreneurial ministry. Here is how he describes this process:

> Coaching and mentoring is a principle and practise that I have adopted for almost 30 years and compliments spiritual direction and soul friendship. Leadership in parochial, Deanery Diocesan, Cathedral and community situations demand coaching and mentoring at every stage, as it impacts local regional and national ministry of the Church. This has been true in developing a new town centre civic church while at the same time being a diocesan advisor in the south west of England, a northern cathedral ministry in a urban setting, minster setting of nine churches in the rural south east of England and presently combining the responsibilities of a large open evangelical church ministering to one of the most deprived communities in Kent.
>
> In 1983, I was introduced to the Coverdale organisation and maintained a working relationship with them until 2001, firstly in being coached and mentored myself and then functioning with them as an assistant coach working with large organisations across the county as well as working in local church and community life on a regular basis. Since 2001 I have had a working relationship with 3D Coaching, which has allowed me to have one-to-one coaching for myself 3 or 4 times a year in order that I may coach and mentor others who are up and coming in leadership potential and practise.
>
> Through open reflection, feedback and dialogue the kernel of learning has developed so that as I approach sabbatical leave in 2013 the conversations of the last decade can be continued. This requires theological reflection, practical planning and collaborative leadership styles in order that succession planning

> for my current post, with all its implications for the next five years, can be worked through thoroughly. This involves cooperation with decision makers, shakers and movers within the present leadership and directorate teams. We also will be pursuing our story by sharing with those who come alongside from other situations across the country how mentoring and coaching can be reciprocated to evolve Christian Ministry in other places.
>
> I am indebted to the coaches and mentors at Coverdale and 3D Coaching who have, who are, and who will continue this dynamic approach to further me as a person in developing potential, affirming skills and creative talents alongside others who are leaders. This develops vision, affirms values, and gives validation that is full of integrity.

Our coaching sessions with John are often reflections on the ongoing work that he is doing all the time. We may meet for four to six hours a year, but that represents many more hours of reflective thinking and prayer. A coaching approach to ministry is the core way John deals with all sorts of things, in a variety of ways, routinely pondering questions such as:

- Where are you using coaching as an integral part of the way you operate as a minister?
- Where do you need external company or challenge from time to time, and how are you making sure you get that?
- Who is developing you?
- Who are you developing in the next generation?

As we see from John's example of preparing for his 2013 sabbatical, the coaching approach means that as you move from one job to another, you leave behind people who are appropriately equipped and confident enough to continue without you. It requires a significantly greater investment of time than doing it all yourself, *and* the rewards are far greater – it is building the Kingdom of God and not the empire of the minister.

Mentoring

A coaching approach is included in mentoring, in spiritual direction, and in pastoral care. Each of these disciplines includes other skills as well. In particular, there can be enormous benefit to using the coaching competency of *contracting* (the International Coach Federation's (ICF) core competency 2: Establishing the Coaching Agreement), by asking questions such as:

- How would you like to use this time today?
- How do you want me to be with you (today)?

It can also be beneficial to change roles within a conversation – *with the consent* of your conversation partner. Many of us have experienced a situation in which a mentor used much of the conversation to talk about themselves. I like to think of mentoring as "I know something you don't know and I'll tell you if you would like me to and if it would be useful," along with a healthy dose of helping the mentee to do much of the work themselves. John takes responsibility for his own learning, discipleship, and development, and is modelling that for those with whom he ministers.

The Bigger Picture

Coaching is so often about the relationship between the coach and the coachee – what do they need to learn, explore, reflect on, or do – that sometimes a coach can forget to return to the big picture. I can remember several conversations with John in which I challenged him about who is capturing the story of ministry where he works so that it can be shared with others – a big demand when you're in a complex parish situation. Yet if we are all part of God's bigger story in our region, our country, and globally, we need to ask the questions:

- What am I learning for me?
- What am I learning for the Kingdom of God?
- What are we learning together – and where does that story need to be told so that others may also learn?

In my last conversation with John, as he reflected on what was happening in his role, I clearly remember thinking, "the place you are standing is holy ground" *(Exodus 5)*. What a privilege to witness! It would serve all of us to ask:

- How do we challenge ourselves and explore the edge of our work, while at the same time acknowledging that we are standing on holy ground?

Long Term

Much of the coaching we do with clergy is short term. We work with them as they discern what might be an appropriate move in ministry and how to engage in applying for a new role. Sometimes we avoid long-term coaching partnerships out of concern that we will lose our edge or begin to collude with the minister. Yet there can be advantages to staying in a coaching partnership for the long term. Consider these questions for your own situation:

- Who decides if the coaching relationship is still working well?
- How long do you need to stay with the person who coaches you? Is it time to move on?
- How will you know if you are maintaining enough of a coaching edge with the people you are coaching?

~~~~~~~~~~~~~~~~~~~~~~~~~

Claire Pedrick is the director of www.3dcoaching.com and is on the faculty of Coaching4Clergy. An experienced coaching supervisor and mentor coach, Claire has been coaching and training clergy for over seventeen years. She is applying for master certified coach (MCC) status with the International Coach Federation. 3D Coaching works with clergy across the whole of England and Wales as well as with public sector leaders. Claire is the co-author of *How to Make Great Appointments in the Church: Calling, Competence and Chemistry.*
~~~~~~~~~~~~~~~~~~~~~~~~~

Taking the Conversation to New Frontiers: Coaching in the Annual Review

By Claire Pedrick

"Well, it was friendly," is a comment too frequently made, or thought, by ministers leaving their annual review conversation. Debbie was more blunt, saying, "I don't know anything that I didn't know before and I could have been using my time more productively." Debbie has a dual role as a hospital chaplain and local minister. It was a great conversation, but her reviewer had only focused on the local church part of the role. For Debbie, the heart of her vocation was her work in the hospital, yet she was too polite to interrupt or try to redirect the conversation.

An annual or biannual review is a necessary but sometimes dreaded event, whether it's with your own staff, your superintendent, a bishop, a regional minister, or clergy for whom you have some pastoral oversight. Too often the reviewer does some preparation beforehand on paper, and the meeting is simply the live movie version of the book. A coaching approach can turn this event into much more than a transactional chat, appraisal, or target-setting session. By negotiating clear boundaries at the beginning of the discussion, the reviewer enables a transformational conversation that can have a positive impact not only on the minister, but also on their congregation and community.

The coaching approach involves so much more than a list of targets and actions. It allows the reviewer to let the Spirit into the details. This approach can help a minister stand back and look at their work and their role from a different perspective. People often describe this as looking at themselves in their ministry from the perspective of a helicopter. Transformation happens when the minister knows or understands something in this new way and a light comes on in their eyes.

In England, my company, 3D Coaching, is training people to use a coaching approach in review conversations. Through supervision and mentor coaching, we support reviewers in developing their practice so that their conversations are transformational. Some of our reviewers have full coaching skills training, but most do not. There are a few key skills that can make all the difference in the way reviewers implement their coaching approach.

Where to Start?

In *The Sound of Music*, Maria sang, "Let's start at the very beginning. It's a very good place to start." This is not true in the case of a review. When you start at the beginning, you can never be sure that there will be enough time for the conversations that need to happen. The review process must begin by looking at what's important to the minister or the church instead of automatically going back to the beginning or the date of the last review.

Neither is the end a helpful starting point; questions that are entirely future-focused risk high-flying dreams and insufficient thought.

So where do you start? There is a Chinese proverb that says, "The banks of the Yangtze give it depth, drive, and direction." It's the boundaries of the review conversation that give it meaning, rather than the open space that is common in so many pastoral conversations.

Here are some ideas about how to start the review conversation by introducing its boundaries:

- How would you like to use this time today?
- What will be a good outcome from this review conversation – [*you can get more specific:*] for you, the church, the parish, the community, the Kingdom of God?

- What would you like to be different by the time you leave?
- How will you know we have done that?
- How would you like me to work with you?
- [And most importantly] Where would you like to start?

Some churches use preparatory documents to help ministers gather their thoughts and gain some focus. Often the reviewer will have sight of these in advance, yet their role is not to ratify or judge but rather to do what needs to be done in order to help the minister do what they need to do.

Sometimes the paperwork reveals a specific issue that the reviewer needs to address. In those cases, a review can't be entirely a coaching-style conversation. Before the reviewer asks the person how he or she wants to start, they can say something like, "There are one or two things from your paperwork that I'd like to discuss."

Our coachees often report that this new style of conversation feels very unfamiliar, but in my experience it is the only way to make sure that the review conversation benefits the minister or staff member, the organization, and the Kingdom. Asking, "What will be a good outcome from this review for the Kingdom of God?" can really create a shift in someone's thinking when they have lost perspective.

Center of Gravity

If you are reviewing the staff in your own church, you will have seen them at work. If you have a regional role and are reviewing a minister, the chances are that you haven't seen the person much in their role in their own church context. Reviews don't work when they are done *to* people. Neither, in fact, do appraisals. They are most effective when we work *together*, and that means the responsibility needs to be between us. That, as you may have discovered, is harder than it sounds.

The most frequent piece of feedback we give to new reviewers when we observe them in training is to *keep the center of gravity in the middle*. As soon as I take responsibility, I am in danger of trying to fix, to solve, to rescue, or to ask questions about some very interesting aspect of ministry that the minister already knows about. Curiosity may be an asset in the process, but it needs to be shared! A regional training officer in the church said to me the other day, "If we can get this right, it will transform the way our ministers work in their context – they will stop taking too much responsibility, too."

The answer to how to do this is simple: When you don't know the right thing to explore next, remember that there are two of you in this dialogue and ask the other person! Helpful questions at this stage might be:

- Where are we now?
- Is this conversation useful? What might we need to do differently?
- Have we gotten to where we need to be?
- We have done X. What do we need to do next?
- [If you have a management role] What do you need to do? What do I need to do?

Get Out of the Way

A minister who attended one of our one-day courses volunteered to sit in the hot seat so that I could demonstrate some of these skills. She wanted to talk about a very complicated situation in her parish in which a number of factions were operating. And she wanted to know what to do next. What do you do when someone asks that? The pastor in you wants to care and support; the problem solver wants to understand enough to be able to make suggestions, and may need lots of detail. And we didn't have long. The minister needed affirmation, understanding of the context, and some possible ways forward.

So we walked to a flip chart and I handed her a pen and said, "Draw what you see." From that moment, with the pen in her hand, she was talking to herself about the problem. She drew stick people and boxes and arrows and lines. My role was to keep asking, "What else can you see?" Each time she had an insight she would draw a line around a box on the bottom left of the page and say, "But it's not about them." Finally I drew a line around a very heavily enclosed box on her sheet and asked, "It's not about them?" And that was the breakthrough – she suddenly saw that the solution was with the people in the box. I know nothing about who did what or said what, because the conversation was about the picture and not the story.

If you want to try this technique, here are a few suggestions to keep in mind:

- Once you have handed over the pen, don't touch it again.
- Stand with the person and look at the picture together.
- Talk about the picture, asking, "what else?" questions.
- Say what you notice.

The same kind of technique can be useful in a challenging conversation with a colleague in your ministry team. When we talk eyeball to eyeball, our companion may resort to a flight or fight response. So use a flip chart or whatever is on hand – pens, post-it notes, even sugar packets if you're at a cafe. One minister's first go at coaching was to use this method to have a conversation with a challenging colleague who needed to move on. The minister told a story with sugar packets: "You have been here for thirty years – the last vicar left and you held the place together for a long time. That was so helpful for the congregation. And [as he brings in a new sugar packet] now I have come in as the leader and I am wondering how that feels for you. I am wondering whether it feels like you have been pushed aside. And I am thinking about how it is for me, needing to take this place forward. And I am wondering what we need to do now."

When you are the one telling the story:

- Tell the story without eye contact.
- Start with "What do *we* need to do?"
- Then move into "What do I/you need to do?"

Real Play

Our experience is that transformation happens when there is a shift in the room – something that you can see – often eye movements or even a jolt. And you can sometimes make that happen. We see it all the time in our coaching training – the moment that coachees (ministers) really understand that there is a conversation they need to have, and what they need to say. Maybe we see a light bulb come on. Maybe we notice them make a note on their pad. Transformation comes when we ask them to pretend that one of us (the trainers) is the person they need to talk to, and then we ask them to stand up and say what they need to say. More often than not, they stop mid-sentence and realize that they need to say something else instead! This is not role-play or rehearsing a script, it is *real play* – simply trying out an idea.

In life we only get one chance at a conversation, especially a difficult one. We then spend many days or weeks – or sometimes years – living with the consequences. Real play gives us the chance to hear our words land before we use them with the real person. It has far more impact than making a list or a script!

~~~~~~~~~~~~~~~~~~~~~~~~~

Claire Pedrick is the director of www.3dcoaching.com and is on the faculty of Coaching4Clergy. An experienced coaching supervisor and mentor coach, Claire has been coaching and training clergy for over seventeen years. She is applying for master certified coach (MCC) status with the International Coach Federation. 3D Coaching works with clergy across the whole of England and Wales as well as with public sector leaders. Claire is the co-author of *How to Make Great Appointments in the Church: Calling, Competence and Chemistry.*
~~~~~~~~~~~~~~~~~~~~~~~~~

Jeremiah 29:11

For I know the plans I have for you, declares the Lord, plans to prosper you and not to harm you, plans to give you hope and a future.

Conclusion

by J. Val Hastings

I want to close this extraordinary book by first telling you what I have learned from pulling together these stories, and where it will take ME and Coaching4Clergy.

I was simply amazed to witness all of the unique and creative ways that coaching is being used in ministry. I knew they were out there, but the compounding effect of reading them one after another really brought it home for me.

Reading this vast variety of real-life stories confirmed the timeless benefits of a coaching approach to ministry. I saw that the Next Great Awakening is underway AND that more and more people in ministry are seeing and using coaching as a way to move into this next season in Christianity.

Being a futurist and a coach, I also find myself wondering, "What's next?" for this movement of God.

Here is what I hope you learned from these stories and where I hope it will take you:

I hope that you've gained a much more solid understanding of coaching and a coaching approach to ministry.

I hope that your curiosity has been piqued to the point of working with your own coach and/or gaining coaching skills for yourself.

I hope that you have seen that while there is much to be concerned about in ministry today, there is also much to celebrate. A new great awakening is happening right in our midst – and we're a part of it!

Is it Time for You to Add Coaching to Your Ministry Toolkit?

As you've read, coaching can be a real blessing to God's people and a valuable way for ministers to:

- resolve conflicts
- lead effectively
- empower individuals in lay ministry and committee work
- energize congregations, and
- shepherd individuals on their walk with God.

Coaching is a practical and Christ-centered tool which can enrich ministry and enhance personal satisfaction.

At Coaching4Clergy, we specialize in equipping ministers with coaching skills through a wide range of coach training courses and programs to meet your ministry needs. Courses are offered in-person or via distance learning.

Visit our website at www.Coaching4Clergy.com to learn more about our coach training options, our global coaching initiative, read our latest articles on the blog, or peruse our free resources.

The Coaching4 Clergy Mission: *Every Pastor, Ministry Staff and Church Leader a Coach.*